Every Sewer's Guide to the Perfect Fit

Every Sewer's Guide to the Perfect Fit

Customizing Your Patterns for a Sensational Look

Mary Morris & Sally McCann

G Street Fabrics

Editor: Kate Mathews
Art Director: Celia Naranjo
Photography: Evan Bracken
Illustrations: Bernadette Wolf
Production Assistant: Bobby Gold
Editorial Assistant: Val Anderson

Library of Congress Cataloging-in-Publication Data
Morris, Mary
      Every sewer's guide to the perfect fit : customizing your patterns
for a sensational look / by Mary Morris and Sally McCann.
        p. cm.
    Includes index.
    ISBN 1-887374-43-4
    1. Dressmaking—Pattern design. 2. Clothing and dress
measurements. 3. Clothing and dress—Alteration. I. McCann, Sally.   II. Title.
TT520.M825   1997
646.4'08—dc21   97.6496
                                        CIP

10 9 8 7 6 5 4 3 2 1

First Edition

Published by Lark Books
50 College St.
Asheville, NC 28801, USA

©1997 Mary Morris and Sally McCann

Distributed by Random House, Inc., in the United States, Canada, the United Kingdom, Europe, and Asia
Distributed in Australia by Capricorn Link (Australia) Pty Ltd., P.O. Box 6651, Baulkham Hills
 Business Centre, NSW 2153, Australia
Distributed in New Zealand by Tandem Press Ltd., 2 Rugby Rd., Birkenhead, Auckland, New Zealand

Printed in Hong Kong by Oceanic Graphic Printing Productions Ltd.

ISBN 1-887374-43-4

Table of Contents

Introduction

"Fitting is too frustrating! I haven't made clothes in years. I stick to slipcovers!"

—*A G Street Fabrics customer*

Why another fitting book? You have answered that question simply by picking up this book. Probably no other problem in sewing, with the possible exception of achieving perfect sewing machine tension, is the source of as much frustration as constructing clothes that fit. Many homesewers have given up altogether, choosing to sew only quilts or home decorating projects. No window or chair has ever been known to change shape while its covering is being sewn or complain about something being too tight, too loose, or making it appear too fat! Many quilters would much rather devote their time and energy to the achievable perfect $^1/_4$-inch (6-mm) seam than attempt to create a bodice that really fits over the bust.

Fitting books often are another source of frustration. They are either overly simplified, offering little help for the average to advanced sewer, or so technical that they remind you of an intimidating high school geometry textbook.

Our experiences—both as sewers of garments and costumes for a wide range of figures, and as teachers and sales assistants at G Street Fabrics near Washington, D.C.—have convinced us that there are few things as disappointing as spending a great deal of money on fabric and hours on cutting, constructing, and finishing a garment only to have it not fit. Good fit is like great taste. Both are immediately recognizable, but each is difficult to define and even harder to teach.

WHAT IS GOOD FIT?

If we were to define good fit in a single sentence, it would probably be somewhat like this:

Good fit is characterized by a garment that follows the shape of the body with no indication of stress or wrinkling; the shoulder seam sitting atop the shoulder; the curves at the neckline, armholes, hips, and waistline following the natural contours of the body without either binding or gapping; and the length of the sleeves and hems being smooth and consistent around the entire width and falling at the most flattering point.

Quite a sentence, isn't it? Its length would make any Victorian novelist proud! However, it makes a very important point: if your garment is uncomfortable and/or has unsightly wrinkles and gaps, it does not fit.

Our system of developing a personal fitting pattern, which will be described in the following pages, has evolved after years of teaching a four-day "Total Fit" workshop at G Street Fabrics. The chapter on pants fitting is based on another workshop entitled "Terrific Pants."

We begin by analyzing commercial fitting patterns, available from almost every

When sewing patterns have been adjusted to fit well, finished garments look better and are more comfortable to wear.

major American and European pattern company. We proceed with careful and exact measurements, a step-by-step method of making alterations that stresses thorough tissue-fitting and recording of adjustments, and the creation and fine-tuning of a fitting muslin (sometimes called a toile). We then explain how to preserve your personal fitting pattern, how to use it to adjust a variety of pattern styles, and how to transform it into a tool for designing your own styles.

Some basic pattern-making skills will be taught, because we do not assume you already have such skills. Each chapter will begin with definitions of basic terms used in that stage of the fitting process, and all procedures and techniques will be clearly illustrated with line drawings and/or photographs.

This system does involve an investment in some basic equipment and a commitment of time from you and a "fitting buddy." This investment, however, will be rewarded many times over with future savings in both time and money. Although some clever individuals, aided by multiple mirrors, extreme physical agility, or a very accurate dress form, may have managed to accurately measure and fit themselves, we highly recommend recruiting a sewing friend

who is as anxious as you are to know how to fit herself accurately. Not only will your fitting buddy's extra set of hands and eyes prove invaluable, you both might have a great deal of fun in the process!

If you do not have a friend who sews and might enjoy being your fitting buddy, you may wish to consult the list of sewing guilds and organizations at the end of this book. Perhaps there is a group in your area that can introduce you to many new sewing friends.

To prepare for this book, we hosted "Misfit Sunday" for the more than 200 employees at G Street Fabrics. The store's employees come from all over the world and represent as many shapes, ages, and sizes as the languages they speak. But they have in common an ability to sew and a love of fine fabric. For Misfit Sunday, we invited them to bring in clothing they had made, but never wear because of fitting problems. You will see photographs of some of these problem garments and how they look after appropriate fitting adjustments were made; the photo captions will explain what the source of the problem was and how the problem was solved. You will be able to see for yourself how the pattern adjustments described in this book improve fitting quality.

Chapter One

Getting started

"Figure? I don't *have a* figure anymore!"

—A still elegant, but mature G Street Fabrics staff member

EVALUATING YOUR FIGURE FOR A GOOD FIT

Before choosing the best fitting pattern for you and adjusting it to be an accurate reflection of your own individual shape, we must consider a number of other factors that affect fit. Good fit begins in front of a full-length mirror. As you stand in front of that mirror, study yourself with an honest, even critical, eye. A 40-something friend and the mother of five grown children once commented that when she looked in a mirror she still saw the 16-year-old girl she once was. As healthy as this may have been for her self-esteem, it would have been counterproductive if she were trying to create clothes that fit her figure as it exists today. Ask for input about your figure from your fitting buddy and tactfully offer your insights about her figure to her.

Checkpoints

• You should first note the general shape of your body. Regardless of your weight, is your body straight, with relatively little difference between your hip and bust measurements and your waist, or curvy, with at least 10 inches (25.5 cm) difference between your waist and your bust and/or hips?

Basic Fitting Terms

ALTERATION LINE. A vertical or horizontal line that indicates the measured distance or space to be altered. It is used in lengthening and shortening, interior alterations, and box method alterations.

ASYMMETRICAL FIGURE. A figure having different measurements at comparable points on different sides of the body, whether from left to right or front to back; also a figure in which the top and bottom are out of proportion to each other.
(See page 12 for more terms.)

• Most pattern companies report that they design patterns for the woman who is 5 feet 6 inches (165 cm) tall. Are you taller or shorter than this?

• Is your body relatively symmetrical from side to side, from top to bottom, and from front to back? As we age, many of us tend to carry more weight in the front at the tummy and bust, and less in the back, especially in the seat.

• Do you have sloping or very rounded shoulders or are they unusually straight or broad?

• Are there any aspects of your figure that strike you as significantly different from the hypothetical statistical average for which patterns are made?

• Do you have especially prominent curves, including one or more of the following: full bust, large abdomen, pronounced seat, or rounded upper back?

• Is your back unusually straight? Do your shoulder blades protrude? Are you swaybacked?

• Do you have either an unusually high or low bust or hip curve?

• When you buy ready-to-wear or sew your own clothes, are they consistently too short or too long in the waist?

When we discuss taking and recording your measurements later on, some of these unique features of your figure may become more evident. Remember: this is a process of figure assessment, not of judgment.

There is no good or bad here, simply reality. You may wish to camouflage, accent, enlarge, or minimize some of the features you discover, but if you truly want to achieve good fit, you must acknowledge them and adjust for their existence.

While honestly taking stock of your figure, do not forget to identify those features and elements you especially like about yourself. You probably will be aware of areas that may require relatively major adjustments. This is the first step toward understanding which styles, regardless of the dictates of fashion, will be most flattering for you. The so-called ideal figure tends to be tall and relatively lean, with shoulders slightly wider than the hips, hip and bust circumferences approximately the same, and waist circumference 10 inches (25.5 cm) smaller. Very few real people match this ideal—even a Barbie doll would fail!

LEARNING TO FLATTER YOUR FIGURE

The first step toward good fit and a result you will like is choosing the correct style for your own very special shape. Remember that vertical seams and fashion details will add height, and tend to slenderize, and that horizontal seams and fashion details will add width. Unusual embellishments, three-dimensional effects (like ruffles), and fabrics that are shiny or brightly colored will tend to draw the eye and accentuate

that part of the garment and figure.

When thumbing through pattern catalogues, most of us are attracted to the photographs of finished garments, but often we can learn much more from the line drawings on the pattern envelope because they clearly show the seams and/or darts that will shape the garment. If you look best and are most comfortable in close-fitting garments, look for patterns with vertical seams and/or darts. The simpler the construction, the more likely the garment is to be semi-fitted or loosely fitted. Note also the suggested fabrics; some designs are meant to be constructed of soft, drapey fabrics, while others call for fabrics (and perhaps underlining, interfacing, or boning) with considerable body, even stiffness. Look with particular care at parts of the garment that you consider to be your problem areas; does the design allow for any camouflage, such as the addition of pads for narrow or sloping shoulders?

ELEMENTS OF GOOD FIT

Now that you have a general notion of your basic shape and points of special concern, think about what constitutes good fit for your figure. Probably the single most common fitting error is making a garment too tight. Very few garments are meant to fit like a second skin. A bathing suit or leotard, strapless gown, and ballerina's tutu bodice are the exceptions. Clothes that are too tight are instantly noticeable to others because of wrinkles and unsightly stress lines, especially at seamlines. The wearer is usually aware of uncomfortable tightness.

The second most common fitting problem is the bust area in dresses and blouses. A bust larger than a B cup creates problems of gapping at armholes, necklines, and front closures. A full bust can also cause the garment to hike up in front. These symptoms are the result of insufficient length and width in the center front of the bodice. In Chapter Five, we will give detailed instructions about how to alter a bodice pattern to correct these problems.

The shoulders are the third area causing fitting concerns. Shoulder pads can compensate for some of the problems associated with this area, especially the need to fill in for sloping and/or narrow shoulders. Broad shoulders, on the other hand, create stress lines that indicate the need for additional room, for the sake of greater comfort and to allow the garment to hang properly.

We will discuss the concept of perfect fit in much more detail in the chapters on the bodice, sleeve, and skirt. We will also look at the special problems of fitting pants. As mentioned above, the Total Fit course at G Street Fabrics takes four full days, with another two-day course devoted to pants fitting.

With you and your fitting buddy working together, you may achieve your goals in less time. Be sure, however, to plan for several significant blocks of time. Working carefully and deliberately now will pay off in rich dividends later.

WHAT YOU NEED TO GET STARTED

The following is a list of supplies you and your fitting buddy will need to have on hand:

1. A commercial fitting pattern in the proper size. Wait to purchase this until after you have taken your measurements. Many of us are surprised to learn that a major reason for our fitting problems is that we have been buying the wrong size pattern!

Vogue offers two versions of a fitting pattern: #1000, which is available in most sizes wherever Vogue patterns are sold, and the more detailed and durable #1001, which may have to be special ordered. Butterick #3415, McCall's #2718, Simplicity #9900, Style #2252, and Burda #3750 are also fitting patterns that are generally kept in stock where each company's patterns are sold. However, they may be special order items in some areas, so check with your sewing pattern dealer. In the following chapter, we will discuss the differences among the typical body shapes for which the major pattern companies design, as well as some of the specific differences among these fitting patterns.

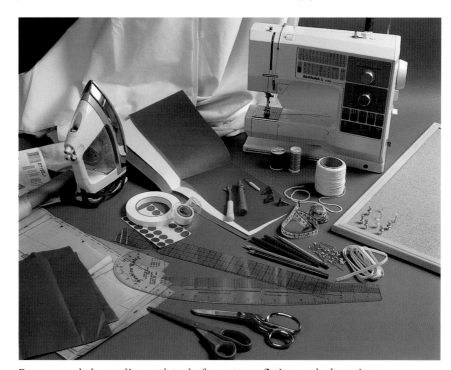

Recommended supplies and tools for pattern fitting and alteration.

Basic Fitting Terms *continued from page 9*

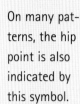

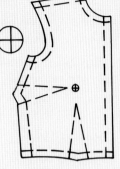

BASIC PATTERN. A plain dress pattern from which style or fashion patterns may be developed, also known as a block, sloper, master, or foundation pattern. Typically, it has center front and back seams or closures, long fitted set-in sleeves, jewel neckline, back shoulder darts, bust darts from the side seam, front and back waist darts in both the bodice and the skirt, waist seam, and straight skirt. In the next chapter, we will discuss features of the basic pattern that differ from those you are accustomed to finding on a typical fashion pattern.

BLENDING (or TRUEING). The process of redrawing the seamline after an adjustment has been made so that it is continuous, if it was broken by the correction process.

BODICE. The upper portion of a dress that has a waist seam.

BUST POINT. The fullest part of the bust curve, sometimes indicated on patterns as a cross in a circle. In this book's diagrams, we will abbreviate it "B.P." and use the conventional symbol, which we suggest you also mark on your pattern if it is not already provided.

SYMBOL:

On many patterns, the hip point is also indicated by this symbol.

COMMERCIAL PATTERN. A pattern made by a professional pattern company.

CROSSWISE GRAIN. The crosswise filler yarns that run back and forth between the selvages at right angles to the lengthwise yarns.

DART. V-shaped seams that shape the garment to the curves of the body. All curved seams are, essentially, darts that have been converted to seams. Darts are a basic method of shaping flat fabric into contoured shapes.

FASHION RULER™. A transparent plastic ruler that is a combination of French curve (see below), hip curve, and straight edge.

FLEXIBLE RULER. Made of a flexible transparent plastic, these rulers come in several sizes, ranging from 1 to 2 inches (2.5 to 5 cm) wide and

from 6 to 24 inches (15 to 61 cm) long. The size best suited to this project is 2 inches (5 cm) wide by 12 inches (30.5 cm) or 18 inches (45.5 cm) long. These rulers are marked with a $\frac{1}{8}$-inch (3-mm) grid across their entire surface, which simplifies the drawing of parallel lines, such as cutting lines, exactly $\frac{5}{8}$ inch (16 mm) from the stitching line. If the ruler does not have a metal edge, its flexibility enables it, when placed on its side, to follow a curved seamline for measuring.

FRENCH CURVE RULER. A pattern-maker's tool made of transparent plastic whose edges are curved to serve as templates for drawing neckline and armhole curves.

GRADING. The process of changing the size of a pattern without altering the underlying design. Although we will make some reference to this process and the techniques graders employ, pattern grading itself is beyond the scope of this book.

GRAINLINE. A line that runs exactly perpendicular to the lengthwise or crosswise yarns in the fabric; usually indicated on the pattern piece by an arrow.

GUIDELINE. A line that is at right angles to a line that is to be slashed. A guideline makes it easier to correctly align two sections during alteration.

HINGE. A ¹/₁₆-inch (1.6-mm) bridge of tissue between two slashes that holds the 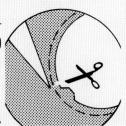 parts of the pattern together while making alterations. Hinges are commonly created along seamlines (not at cutting lines), at dart points, or at the bust point. Once a hinge has been created, parts of the pattern can be rotated or pivoted without creating bulges in the tissue.

HIP CURVE. The shape of the side edge of the body between the waistline and the fullest part of the hip; a hip curve ruler or Fashion Ruler imitates the various shapes this curve might take so the pattern-maker can duplicate it.

HORIZONTAL. Running crosswise, from side to side; parallel with the horizon. The bustline, hipline, and hemline are usually parallel to the floor. The waistline, although basically horizontal, may not be exactly parallel because it is usually curved.

LENGTHWISE GRAIN. The lengthwise threads of the fabric, parallel to the selvages.

PATTERN ADJUSTMENT, CORRECTION, or ALTERATION. A change in the shape of the pattern to reflect the individual's measurements.

PERSONAL BASIC or FITTING PATTERN. A basic pattern that has been adjusted to an individual's measurements. It is a close-fitting garment with a waistline seam and darts in the bodice, skirt, and sleeve. The skirt has straight lines and the sleeve is fitted.

PIVOT POINT. The point from which darts radiate. This is also the point at which hinges are often created when darts are altered or moved.

←PIVOT POINT

SEAM ALLOWANCE. Amount of fabric allowed beyond the seamline or stitching line for joining garment sections.

SELVAGE. The factory-finished edge of the fabric.

SHIFT or SHEATH DRESS. A dress without a waistline. Sheaths tend to be closely fitted, while shifts may have a more relaxed fit.

SLASH. To cut accurately along an alteration line.

SLOPER. The basic pattern used by commercial pattern companies and in the ready-to-wear industry to create other patterns.

SQUARE A LINE. To draw a line at a right angle to another.

TRUEING. See BLENDING.

VERTICAL. A line running from top to bottom, often (but not always) at a right angle to the horizontal.

Do you feel as though you are back in that high school geometry class? Don't worry—there won't be a pop quiz. Leave a marker in these pages so you can refer back to the definitions, if need be. We promise that you will soon be using these words with great confidence!

2. Dressmaker's shears.

3. Scissors for cutting paper.

4. Tape: transparent, **removable** tape; $^1/_2$ or $^3/_4$ inch (1.25 or 2 cm) are the recommended widths. By the time you are finished, you may wonder how you ever functioned without this!

5. Optional tape: $^1/_2$-inch (1.25-cm) masking tape and/or stick-on removable dots to assist in marking and measuring (usually available in any drug, stationery, or office supply store).

6. Straight pins: we find the glass-headed type easier to work with and much easier to find when we drop them.

7. Tracing wheel and paper.

8. Pencil with eraser.

9. Colored pencils, at least two additional colors besides the conventional gray graphite, and at least one color of a narrow point flow pen.

10. French curve or Fashion Ruler™ (see Basic Fitting Terms).

11. Hip curve or Fashion Ruler™.

12. Approximately 6 yards (5.5 m) of 45-inch (1.1-m) wide pre-washed grain-perfect muslin for the dress, to allow for re-cutting, if necessary; and approximately 4 yards (3.7 m) additional for the pants

13. Thread for construction of muslin dress and pants.

14. Several sheets of colored tissue paper.

15. Rulers: 12-inch (30.5-cm) or 18-inch (45.5-cm) flexible, transparent with $^1/_8$-inch (3-mm) grid and **without** a metal edge

16. Seamstress's tape measure

17. 4 or 5 yards (3.7 or 4.6 m) of $^1/_4$-inch (6-mm) elastic

18. A sewing machine for each of you.

19. A cork, foam core, or pinnable cutting mat for each of you. You will pin pattern pieces onto this board as you make needed adjustments.

20. A cardboard tube, such as the type that extra wide foil and wrapping paper come on, on which to store your fitting pattern to keep it wrinkle-free.

21. Common string and weights to serve as plumb lines. To create the precisely vertical or "plumb" lines needed for assessing side seams and comparing your front and back proportions, cut a piece of household string long enough to reach from your shoulder to your knee plus 4 inches (10 cm). Tie a pencil, fishing weight, or other weight to one end.

22. Iron and ironing board.

23. Full-length mirror.

24. Seam ripper (we cannot always achieve perfection on the first attempt!)

You and your fitting buddy must be appropriately dressed for taking measurements and for pin-fitting both the tissue and muslin. Long-sleeved leotards are ideal, providing you are wearing the proper foundation garments underneath. A full slip also works well, except for taking the pants crotch measurements. It is essential that you wear the exact foundation garments you normally wear under a fitted dress. Bathing suits are less suitable since their padding and boning often distort actual measurements.

GENERAL PATTERN ALTERATION METHODS

As you analyze your figure and consider which alterations may be necessary, you may notice that adjustments generally fall into three categories—length, circumference or width, and the curves in rounded areas such as the shoulders, bust, hip, abdomen, and seat. If you have worked with multi-sized patterns, you have probably observed where the greatest changes are made to increase or decrease the size of the garment. Adjustments in width tend to be concentrated more along side seams than center seams, for instance. You may also have noted that larger sizes, although not intended for taller women, tend to allow additional length to cover the more generous curves of the wearer. See? You know more than you thought you did. All of these observations have already prepared you to take the important next step to a higher level of sewing expertise.

Some of the alteration procedures or methods you will use are common to all pattern adjustments, while others are particular to the specific adjustment required. A brief review of these procedures should be especially helpful to readers who have little or no previous experience with pattern alteration.

Blending or Trueing Seamlines and Cutting Lines

This procedure is used in almost every alteration you will make. It involves both a term and a tool—blending or trueing an altered seamline, using the French curve, Fashion Ruler, hip curve, or straight ruler. Blending a straight seamline that has been altered is relatively simple: use the transparent ruler or the straight edge of the Fashion Ruler to draw a new straight line that connects the beginning and ending points of the new seam. See Figure 1.

Blending a curved seamline that has been changed is a bit trickier, but it's a skill that develops quickly with a little practice. Once you learn this method, you will be a blending pro! When a seam is altered, a "jog" or area of unevenness occurs in both the stitching and cutting lines. To blend or true the seam and eliminate the jog, follow these steps:

1. Locate the midpoint of the jog and mark it with a dot.

2. Blend through the mark along the seamline in both directions, back to the original line—above and below the alteration. The new seamline should be continuous and free of any waviness. See Figure 1. To

guide you, use the French curve, hip curve, or the portion of the Fashion Ruler that most closely resembles the curve you are attempting to blend.

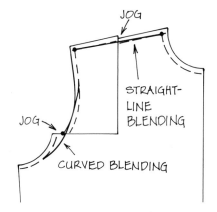

Figure 1. Blending straight and curved seamlines.

3. Make needed corrections to the seam allowance and cutting lines.

Methods for Lengthening/Shortening

If you have been sewing for any length of time, you have already picked up the rudiments of pattern adjustment, perhaps without realizing it. Almost all commercial patterns come marked with lines to indicate where bodices, skirts, pants, sleeves, and hems can be shortened or lengthened.

To shorten the pattern, you have usually followed these steps:

1. Determine the amount you need to shorten. Measure the needed distance above or below the lengthen/shorten line on the pattern and draw an alteration line parallel to the one provided on the pattern.

2. Draw a guideline at a right angle to the lengthen/shorten line or extend the grainline.

3. Slash along the lengthen/ shorten line, separating the pattern into two parts.

4. Place the pattern parts onto the cork or foam core mat; slide and overlap the pattern pieces to the alteration line. This is called the "slash and slide" method.

5. Pin and tape the alteration into place. Blend seamlines and cutting lines, and redraw darts as necessary.

6. An alternative method eliminates the need to cut the pattern in two: fold along the lengthen/ shorten line, creating a tuck. See Figure 2.

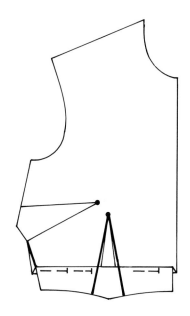

Figure 2. Shortening a pattern piece by folding along the lengthen/ shorten line.

To lengthen a pattern, you have probably used a similar procedure, following these steps:

1. Draw a guideline at a right angle to the lengthen/shorten line or extend the grainline.

2. Slash along the lengthen/shorten line.

3. Place the two pattern pieces over a fresh piece of tissue paper; pin and then tape the cut edge of one pattern piece to the tissue.

4. Determine the amount you need to lengthen, and measure that distance away from the taped edge, and draw an alteration line on the tissue, parallel to the cut edge; extend the guideline or grainline across the tissue.

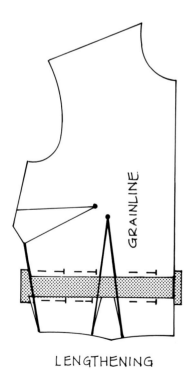

Figure 3. Lengthening a pattern piece with the slash and slide method.

5. Match the cut edge of the second pattern piece to the alteration line you have drawn, taking care to align seamlines and guideline or grainline. See Figure 3.

6. Pin and tape in place. Blend seamlines and redraw darts as necessary.

These two "slash and slide" methods that are already so familiar to you are classified as minor alterations. When you make these or any other corrections, you will place the pattern pieces and the tissue, if needed, on the cork or foam core mat and pin one part of the pattern piece to the mat, leaving the other free to be manipulated. This procedure will assure greater accuracy and will preserve the pattern from unnecessary damage.

Methods for Adding or Subtracting Width

Most homesewers have, on occasion, used this first method—adding or subtracting width at the side seams. This is called an "exterior correction" and is considered a minor alteration. The steps to follow are:

1. Determine the amount of alteration needed at the front and back bust, waist, front high hip, or low back hip. The Personal Measurement Chart you will complete in Chapter Three will make this process much easier.

2. Measure in or out from the side seam the required amount and make

a mark. On the bodice, make marks to adjust for both bust and waist. On the skirt, make marks to adjust for both waist and hip; to preserve the line of the skirt, you must also make a mark at the hemline the same distance from the seamline as you have at the hipline.

3. Fold any darts closed and redraw the seamlines, making straight lines for the side bodice seam and side skirt seam from hipline to hemline. See Figure 4.

4. Use the hip curve and/or Fashion Ruler to redraw the hip seamline. For a high hip curve, use the curvy end of the ruler; for a lower curve, use the flatter side of the ruler. Begin drawing the new curve at the waist and continue down the side of the skirt.

If you have been a very courageous homesewer, you may have used this second method—folding a tuck or slashing/overlapping to subtract width or spreading apart to add width. This method is very similar to the slash and slide technique you used to add or subtract length; the difference is that the slash or fold line you create is now vertical rather than horizontal. This method of width adjustment is called an "interior alteration." Because it affects two areas of the pattern, it is considered a major alteration, despite the fact that it is relatively easy—even if it is a bit scary to perform. Using a skirt front as an example, follow these steps to add or subtract width:

1. Determine the exact amount of width adjustment needed across the waist and hip of the skirt front. You will make this calculation when filling out the Personal Measurement Chart in Chapter Three.

2. Draw a vertical slash or fold line from the waist seam to the hemline, about 1 1/2 inches (4 cm) in from the side seam and parallel to the grainline; the line should not interfere with any darts. See Figure 5.

3. Draw a guideline at a right angle to the slash line or use the lengthen/shorten line as a guideline.

To subtract width:

1. Draw an alteration line the needed amount away from and parallel to the first line; again, this line should not interfere with any darts.

2. Slash along the original line; slide the cut edge over to the alteration line, and align the guideline.

3. Pin and tape in place; blend waist seamline and hemline.

To add width:

1. Cut along the slash line and place the two parts of the pattern over tissue on the cork or foam core mat; pin and tape one part in place.

2. On the tissue, draw an alteration line the needed distance away from and parallel to the taped cut edge.

3. Extend the hipline or guideline across the tissue.

4. Move the second pattern piece away from the taped cut edge to the alteration line, matching the guide-

lines to keep the cut edges exactly parallel to one another.

5. Pin and tape the second pattern part to the tissue; blend waist seamline and hemline.

Adjustments for Curved Areas

Alterations to prominent curves often involve more than one area of the body. For example, adjusting the armhole curve may affect the back, front, and shoulder areas. Three different alteration methods can be used to alter curves; the one you choose will depend on the size of the needed adjustment and whether you need to adjust more than one area at a time.

The slash and pivot method

This method can be a minor alteration when used to alter the length of the shoulder seam. It can also be a major alteration if both length and width must be adjusted over a prominent curve, such as the bust, abdomen, back, and seat. This method requires slashing through darts and other lines, and spreading or overlapping the parts of the pattern. These corrections will be described in detail in the specific chapters relating to various sections of the garment.

The wedge slash and pivot method

This method is considered a minor alteration and is not used to adjust for prominent curves. Use it if you need to adjust only the

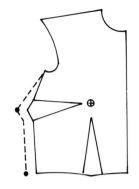

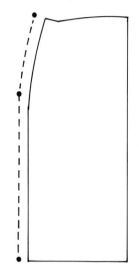

Figure 4. Adding width at the side seams.

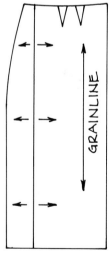

Figure 5. Adding or subtracting width along a slash line from waist to hem.

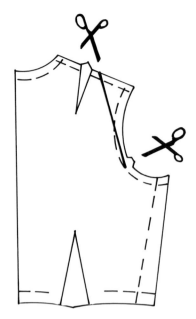

Figure 6. The wedge slash and pivot method to alter shoulder seam length.

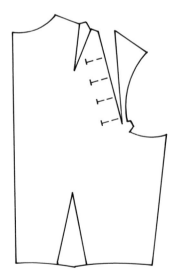

Figure 7. Shoulder seam is lengthened by opening wedge along slash to armhole hinge.

length of the shoulder seam, leaving the chest area relatively unaffected. Follow these steps:

1. Make a mark on the shoulder seam 1 1/2 inches (4 cm) in from the shoulder point.

2. Make a second mark on the armhole seam opposite the notches.

3. Draw a diagonal line between the two marks.

4. Slash along the line through the shoulder seam allowance to, but not through, the second mark at the armhole seam. See Figure 6.

5. Clip through the armhole seam allowance to, but not through, the second mark, creating a hinge.

6. To shorten the shoulder seam, make a mark the needed distance toward the neckline from the diagonal slash. Pin the hinge to the cork or foam core mat and along the inside edge of the slash. Pivot the outer part of the pattern until the slash overlaps and meets the mark. The overlapped correction will resemble a wedge. Pin and tape in place, keeping the pattern flat. Redraw a straight shoulder seamline.

7. To add length to the shoulder seam, draw and slash along the same line as described above. Pin the hinge to the cork or foam core mat and along the inside edge of the slash. Pivot the slash open. The needed addition will resemble a wedge; it will be widest at the shoulder and will taper to the armhole seam. See Figure 7. Add tissue;

pin and tape in place; redraw a straight shoulder seamline.

The L-slash method

The L-slash method is used to alter two or more areas, such as shoulder seam length and chest width, that are in the vicinity of a curved seam, such as the armhole. Follow these steps:

1. Make a mark on the shoulder seam 1 to 1 1/2 inches (2.5 to 4 cm) in from the armhole seam.

2. Draw a vertical slash line from this mark down to a level opposite the armhole notches.

3. Square a line from the end of the slash line over to the armhole edge.

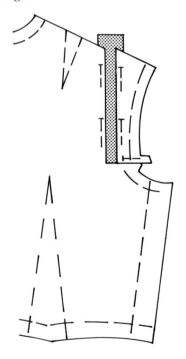

Figure 8. L-slash method to alter shoulder seam length and chest or back width.

4. Slash along both lines; draw the alteration line parallel to the vertical slash line.

5. Slide the L-section in or out, inserting tissue as needed. See Figure 8. NOTE: If you need to move the position of the entire armhole, extend the vertical slash line down below the armhole and square the second line to the side seam. See Figure 9.

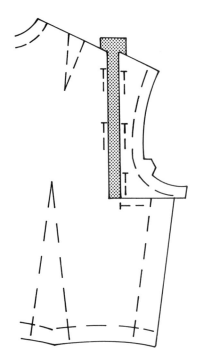

Figure 9. L-slash method to alter armhole position as well as shoulder seam length.

6. Blend shoulder and armhole seamlines and cutting lines as needed. Remember that whatever change you make to the front shoulder must also be made to the back shoulder.

You now have a choice between two methods of altering the shoulder seam: the wedge and pivot, which changes only shoulder length, or the L-slash, which alters the area below as well. Regardless of the method you choose, the same alteration in shoulder length must be made to both the front and back. You can, however, use the L-slash in front, if the chest also must be altered, and the wedge in back, if the upper back does not need any change.

The box method

This alteration technique is similar to the L-slash and is commonly used to correct one specific area. To use the box method to alter the back width, for example, without affecting either the height of the armhole or the length or height of the shoulder seam, follow these steps:

1. Draw a horizontal line from the armhole seam at the notch 1$\frac{1}{2}$ to 2 inches (4 to 5 cm) into the interior of the pattern.

2. Draw a second line, parallel to the first and approximately 2 inches (5 cm) below the shoulder point.

3. Square a line to the two end points of the previous lines, to form a box; the armhole seamline is the fourth side of the box.

4. Cut along all three lines you drew. Draw the alteration line parallel to the vertical side of the box and slide the box in or out the necessary distance, adding tissue if needed. See Figure 10.

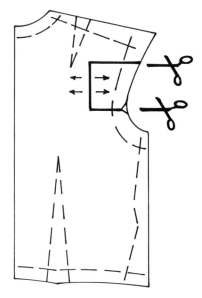

Figure 10. Box method to alter back width.

5. Blend armhole seamline and cutting line as needed.

As you go through the process of adjusting the fitting pattern, we will review these procedures again. So warm up the teapot or ice the lemonade. Break out the cookies (low-fat, of course) or the raw veggies and dip, and invite your fitting buddy over. You are ready to begin.

Chapter Two

Understanding and comparing fitting patterns

EVALUATING THE COMMERCIAL FITTING PATTERNS

The first decision you will confront as you develop your personal fitting pattern is which of the commercial fitting patterns to use as a starting point. One consideration is the availability of a given pattern in your area. Another consideration is the company whose patterns you generally choose when making a garment for yourself. Often, we have found ourselves returning to the same company because its styles and general fit seem to be best for us.

All the major American companies use the same basic body measurements, and the European patterns vary only slightly. As you may have noticed, there is no such consistency among ready-to-wear clothing manufacturers. In fact, over the years, "pattern creep" has resulted in a given ready-to-wear size becoming larger and larger, perhaps to flatter every consumer into thinking she can wear a smaller size. In most cases, you will need to buy a pattern at least one size larger than you wear in ready-to-wear. Depend-ing on the quality and brands of clothing you customarily buy, there may be an even greater difference. Remember—there are no size labels in clothing you sew. People will never know what size pattern you use, but they will notice if the resulting garment does not fit.

Despite the general uniformity of body measurements among pattern companies, however, there are significant differences. How can this be? One reason is the different amount of fitting ease each pattern company allows and the slight variations in length, neck and shoulder curves and angles, and waistline shapes they have adopted. On the following pages, you will see the bodice, sleeve, and skirt pattern pieces from the major American pattern companies (Vogue/Butterick, Simplicity, McCall's), Simplicity's English pattern company (Style), and the best-known German company (Burda). Although they are all the same size (10), you can see that there is considerable variation among them.

For example, the European Burda and Style skirt patterns are designed for

Basic Fitting Terms

ARMHOLE POINT. The point at which the armhole seamline and side bodice seamline meet. Abbreviation: A.P.

ARMSCYE. The curve of the seamline around the armhole.

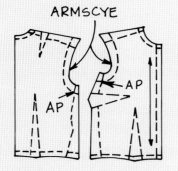

ARMSCYE

AP
AP

BUST DARTS or SIDE DARTS. The darts running almost horizontally from the side seam toward the fullest part of the bust.

BUSTLINE or FULL BUST. The line drawn horizontally on the fitting pattern through the bust point just along the top of the bust dart and across the back.

CAP LINE or BICEP LINE. A horizontal line drawn across the base of the sleeve cap on a fitting pattern that joins the armhole points on either side of the sleeve pattern.

CAP OF SLEEVE. The curved portion of the sleeve above the armhole points, cap line, or bicep line.

CENTER LINE. The line indicated on both fitting and fashion patterns where the front and back center of the garment should be; especially important if there is a closure or an overlapping fashion detail.

CIRCLE. The mark on patterns that conventionally indicates the point on a seam where it will meet another seam, as at the top of the sleeve cap.

CIRCUMFERENCE. The "distance around." When you are working with the bodice and the skirt, the pattern pieces represent only one quarter of the total distance around the body at any point. Therefore, you must take front-plus-back-times-two to equal the whole circumference.

DOT. A small circle that is filled in; it is frequently used in the alteration process to assure accuracy.

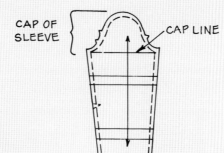

CAP OF
SLEEVE

CAP LINE

DESIGN EASE. The extra fabric, over and above fitting ease, that the designer adds to a garment to change its basic line and shape.

EASE ALLOWANCE. At its most basic, extra fabric.

EASE (verb). The process of gently gathering a longer piece of fabric when sewing it to a shorter one, to create sufficient shaping for the garment to go over curved portions of the body, particularly the bust, the shoulder blades, and in the sleeve cap to accommodate the curve of the shoulder.

FITTING EASE. The extra fabric allowed over and above the body measurements to ensure comfort, ease of movement, and smoothness in a garment.

HIGH BUST (sometimes called UPPER CHEST). A measurement taken under the armhole and just above the bust itself. Abbreviation: H.B. This is the truest indication of the proper size pattern you should buy for a dress, top, or fitting pattern, especially if you wear a C cup bra or larger.

HIGH HIPLINE. A location on a fitting pattern about 3 inches (7.5 cm) below the side waist point or just below the front darts. The high hipline serves as yet another reference point for determining the shape and placement of your hip curve.

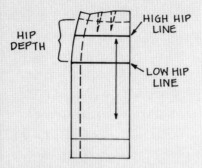

HIP DEPTH. The length along your side hip curve to the fullest part of your hip. On most patterns the low hipline falls 8½ to 9 inches (21.5 to 23 cm) below the waistline as measured along the side seam.

LAYOUT. The arrangement of the pattern pieces on the fabric before cutting.

LOW HIPLINE or HIPLINE. A horizontal line drawn across the skirt front and back that usually indicates the point of greatest fullness in the hips.

NAPE OF NECK. The point where a jewel neckline would fall at the center back, usually at the bone between the neck and spine.

NECK POINT. The point at which the neck seamline and shoulder seamline meet. Abbreviation: N.P.

NOTCHES. The triangular marks along cutting lines that help you match seams correctly. The notches along the armhole seam, both in the bodice and the sleeve, usually indicate the point at which the armhole crease is visible when the arms are hanging comfortably at the sides. Notches can be single, double, or triple. Double notches usually indicate the back of a garment, such as the back of the sleeve.

SEAMLINE or STITCHING LINE (on a pattern). A broken line some distance in from the cutting line, indicating where the seam should be sewn. Seldom indicated on modern fashion patterns, they are marked on some fitting patterns because seam allowances in this case may vary greatly, to allow for necessary adjustments. If your fitting pattern indicates that only the ⅝-inch (16-mm) seam allowance generally used in sewing has been included, we suggest you add extra seam allowance by extending it beyond the cutting line indicated on the pattern. Add seam allowances up to 1 inch

(2.5 cm) at the side seams and waist seams of bodices and skirts, shoulder seams, and the top of the sleeve cap.

SHOULDER POINT. The point at which the shoulder seamline and the armhole seamline meet, often indicated by a circle or dot on the sleeve cap. Abbreviation: SH.P.

SIDE WAIST POINT. The point at which the side seamlines of both the skirt and the bodice meet the waistline.

WAIST DARTS. The darts that run vertically from the waistline. In the bodice they point toward the fullest part of the bust in front and toward the shoulder blades in back. In the skirt front, they point down and around the curve of the tummy and, in the back, down toward the fullest part of the seat. There are usually two darts on each side of the skirt back and often two darts on each side of the skirt front.

WAISTLINE. The indentation around the center of the torso to which a piece of slightly stretched elastic naturally gravitates. The waistline is usually, but not always, horizontal.

slightly shorter waisted, more curvy individuals than are the Simplicity, Vogue/Butterick, and McCall's patterns. Therefore, they are especially suited to women with a relatively high hip curve, since there is less distance between the waistline and the fullest part of the hip. On the other hand, the additional ease in the hip area on a McCall's or Simplicity pattern means that individuals with the very common inverted triangle figure (hips proportionately larger than bust and shoulders), would have less adjustment to make.

We were curious to see exactly how these patterns compare, so we measured the distances between the seamlines at key areas of size 10 fitting patterns from each of these companies. The charts on pages 25–29, indicate our findings. NOTE: All the companies state that their patterns are designed for women 5 feet 6 inches (165 cm) tall.

Comparing specific pattern pieces from the various companies reveals other differences among the front bodices and skirt backs or fronts. Neckline and armscye curves differ, as do waist and hip curves. Some patterns have center front seams in both the bodice and the skirt, while others do not. The number of waist darts in the skirt also differs among the patterns.

These design differences may affect your choice of fitting pattern. Double waist darts on either side of the skirt front and back allow for greater flexibility, especially if there is a significant difference between your waist measurement and your hip measurement, and if your abdomen or seat are especially prominent. If your shoulders are significantly sloping, straight, narrow, or wide, look closely at the differences in the length measurement and the angle of the shoulder seam. The upper chest measurement and the back width might also be important keys if your back is unusually wide, narrow, or rounded.

Vogue #1000 and #1001, McCall's #2718, and Simplicity #9900 provide separate front bodice pattern pieces for A, B, C, and D cups; and Butterick #3415 provides a lower bodice template to allow for these differences. Vogue #1001, which is essentially an entire dress pattern (right and left as well as front and back) printed on gridded non-woven lining fabric, is perfect for someone whose figure is asymmetrical from left to right, because each side can be adjusted and fitted separately. If your figure fits this description but you prefer one of the other patterns, you simply have to make duplicate tissue copies of each pattern piece and transfer all markings so that the duplicates are mirror images of those that came with the pattern.

When we teach the "Total Fit" classes at G Street Fabrics, we ask all participants to use Vogue #1000, both for the sake of consistency and because this pattern is typically an in-stock item, has especially generous seam allowances, and has all seamlines and key reference points and measurement lines pre-marked. To teach students how to make the bust cup adjustments they will have to make on fashion patterns (since all fashion patterns are designed to fit a B cup), however, we have everyone work with the B cup bodice pattern piece.

Because you may not always work with the same pattern company as the one that made your fitting pattern, and we have already seen that there are some significant differences among the companies' patterns, it is very important that you understand how and why to make needed changes—especially the bust change, if it is required. Even with multi-sized patterns, bust cup changes are necessary. Therefore, we recommend that you also work with a B cup fitting pattern.

Once your fitting pattern is completely customized, you will preserve it—changes and all. This will act as a template to be compared with your fashion pattern. It will also serve as a quick reference showing you exactly how to make needed adjustments and can be used for pattern-making.

You will also make a muslin dress from this pattern and may find the need for further fine-tuning based on how the muslin looks and feels.

(Continued on page 30.)

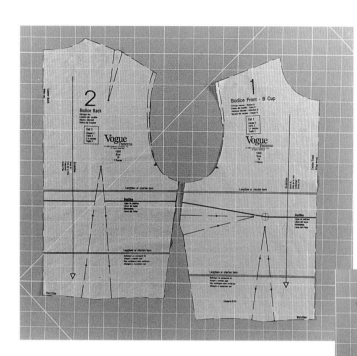

Bodice front and back from Vogue #1000 fitting pattern, by permission of The Butterick Co., Inc., New York, NY.

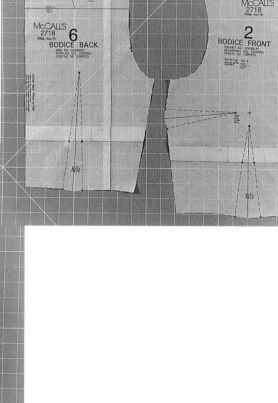

Bodice front and back from McCall's #2718 fitting pattern, by permission of Palmer/Pletsch and The McCall Pattern Company, New York, NY.

Bodice front and back from Simplicity #9900 fitting pattern, by permission of Simplicity Pattern Co., Inc., New York, NY.

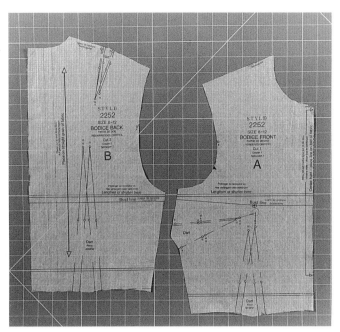

Bodice front and back from Style #2252 fitting pattern, by permission of Simplicity Pattern Co., Inc., New York, NY.

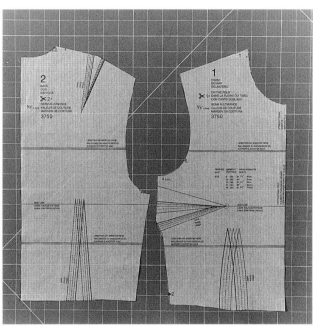

Bodice front and back from Burda #3750 fitting pattern, by permission of Burda Patterns, Inc., Marietta, GA.

	Vogue #1000–1 Butterick #3415	McCall's #2718	Simplicity #9900	Style #2252	Burda #3750
Bust (Pattern)	35" (89 cm)	36" (91.5 cm)	36³/₄" (93.5 cm)	36" (91.5 cm)	36³/₄" (93.5 cm)
Bust (Body)	32¹/₂" (82.5 cm)	32¹/₂" (82.5 cm)	32¹/₂" (82.5 cm)	32¹/₂" (82.5 cm)	33" (84 cm)
Bust Ease	2¹/₂" (6.5 cm)	3¹/₂" (9 cm)	4¹/₄" (11 cm)	3¹/₂" (9 cm)	3³/₄" (9.5 cm)
Waist (Pattern)	25¹/₂" (64.75 cm)	26⁵/₈" (67.75 cm)	26³/₄" (68 cm)	26¹/₂" (67.5 cm)	26³/₄" (68 cm)
Waist (Body)	25" (63.5 cm)	25" (63.5 cm)	25" (63.5 cm)	25" (63.5 cm)	26" (66 cm)
Waist Ease	¹/₂" (1.25 cm)	1⁵/₈" (4.25 cm)	1³/₄" (4.5 cm)	1¹/₂" (4 cm)	³/₄" (2 cm)
Back Neck to Waist (Pattern)	16 ³/₈" (42 cm)	16¹/₈" (41 cm)	16³/₈" (42 cm)	16¹/₄" (41.5 cm)	16" (40.5 cm)
Nape of Neck to Bust Point	14¹/₂" (37 cm)	13⁷/₈" (35.25 cm)	14¹/₂" (37 cm)	14" (35.5 cm)	13⁷/₈" (35.25 cm)
Bust Point to Center Front	7³/₄" (19.5 cm)	7⁵/₈" (19.25 cm)	8" (20.5 cm)	7¹/₂" (19 cm)	8" (20.5 cm)
Shoulder Seam Length	4³/₄–5¹/₄" (12–13.5 cm)	4³/₄" (12 cm)	5" (12.5 cm)	5¹/₄" (13.5 cm)	5" (12.5 cm)
Back Width	14¹/₂" (37 cm)	14¹/₄" (36 cm)	16" (40.5 cm)	15" (38 cm)	14³/₄" (37.5 cm)

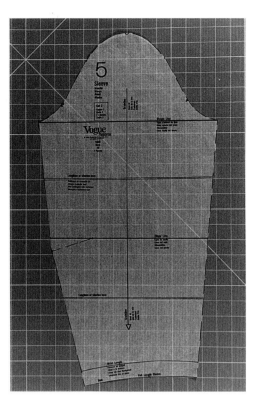

Sleeve from Vogue #1000 fitting pattern, by permission of The Butterick Co., Inc., New York, NY.

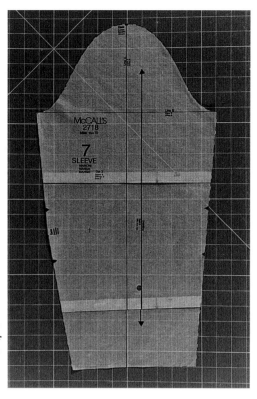

Sleeve from McCall's #2718 fitting pattern, by permission of Palmer/Pletsch and The McCall Pattern Company, New York, NY.

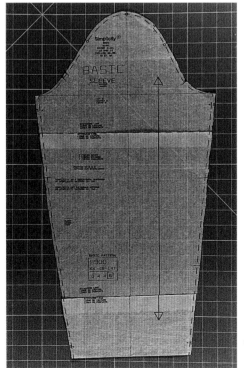

Sleeve from Simplicity #9900 fitting pattern, by permission of Simplicity Pattern Co., Inc., New York, NY.

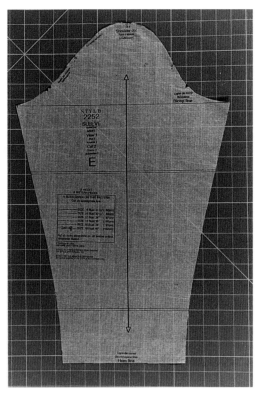

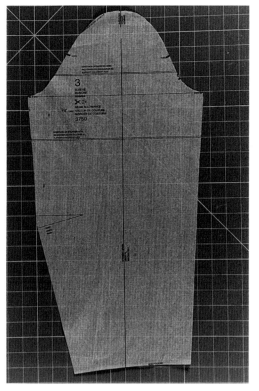

Sleeve from Style #2252 fitting pattern, by permission of Simplicity Pattern Co., Inc., New York, NY.

Sleeve from Burda #3750 fitting pattern, by permission of Burda Patterns, Inc., Marietta, GA.

	Vogue #1000–1 Butterick #3415	McCall's #2718	Simplicity #9900	Style #2252	Burda #3750
Sleeve Cap Height	6" (15 cm)	5⁷/8" (14.75 cm)	5⁵/8" (14.25 cm)	5¹/2" (14 cm)	5⁵/8" (14.25 cm)
Seam around Sleeve Cap	18¹/4" (46.5 cm)	17⁵/8" (44.75 cm)	18" (45.5 cm)	19¹/2" (49.5 cm)	18" (45.5 cm)
Bicep	12¹/4" (31 cm)	12 ³/8" (39 cm)	12³/4" (32.5 cm)	14¹/2" (37 cm)	12¹/8" (30.75 cm)
A.P. to Elbow	7³/4" (19.5 cm)	8¹/8" (20.75 cm)	8¹/4" (21 cm)	n.a.	8" (20.5 cm)
Elbow to Wrist	8¹/4" (21 cm)	9 ¹/8" (23.25 cm)	9¹/2" (24 cm)	n.a.	10" (25.5 cm)
SH.P. to Wrist	22" (56 cm)	22³/4" (58 cm)	22³/4" (58 cm)	22³/4" (58 cm)	23³/4" (60.5 cm)

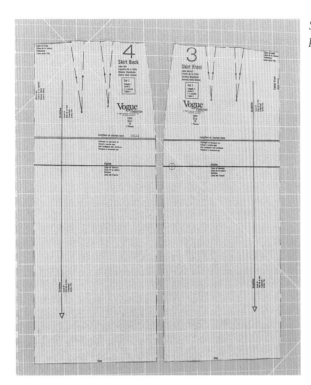

Skirt front and back from Vogue #1000 fitting pattern, by permission of The Butterick Co., Inc., New York, NY.

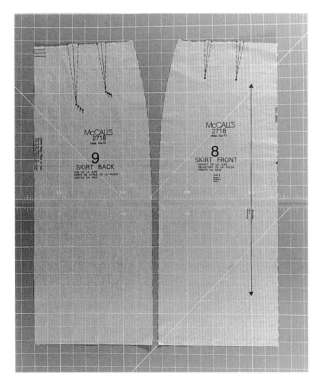

Skirt front and back from McCall's #2718 fitting pattern, by permission of Palmer/Pletsch and The McCall Pattern Company, New York, NY.

Skirt front and back from Simplicity #9900 fitting pattern, by permission of Simplicity Pattern Co., Inc., New York, NY.

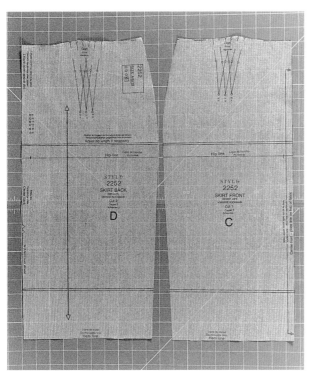

Skirt front and back from Style #2252 fitting pattern, by permission of Simplicity Pattern Co., Inc., New York, NY.

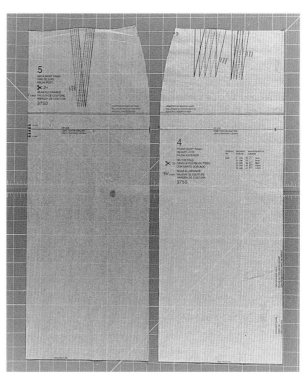

Skirt front and back from Burda #3750 fitting pattern, by permission of Burda Patterns, Inc., Marietta, GA.

	Vogue #1000–1 Butterick #3415	McCall's #2718	Simplicity #9900	Style #2252	Burda #3750
Low Hip (Pattern)	36$\frac{1}{2}$" (92.5 cm)	36$\frac{3}{4}$" (93.5 cm)	37$\frac{3}{4}$" (96 cm)	36" (91.5 cm)	36$\frac{3}{4}$" (93.5 cm)
Low Hip (Body)	34$\frac{1}{2}$" (87.5 cm)	34$\frac{1}{2}$" (87.5 cm)	34$\frac{1}{2}$" (87.5 cm)	34$\frac{1}{2}$" (87.5 cm)	35$\frac{1}{2}$" (90 cm)
Low Hip Ease	2" (5 cm)	2$\frac{1}{4}$" (6 cm)	3$\frac{1}{4}$" (8.5 cm)	1$\frac{1}{2}$" (4 cm)	1$\frac{1}{4}$" (3.5 cm)
Waist to Hipline (Pattern)	9" (23 cm)	9$\frac{3}{4}$" (25 cm)	9$\frac{3}{4}$" (25 cm)	8$\frac{1}{2}$" (21.5 cm)	7$\frac{3}{4}$" (19.5 cm)
Center Front to Hem	22$\frac{7}{8}$" (58 cm)	22$\frac{3}{4}$" (57.75 cm)	29$\frac{1}{2}$" (75 cm)	21" (53.5 cm)	23$\frac{5}{8}$" (60 cm)

(Continued from page 23.)

These small adjustments will then be transferred to your fitting pattern and to the Personal Measurement Chart you will fill out in the next chapter. Unless you experience a significant weight change or a number of years pass, you will probably find that, except when working with an unusual design or especially delicate and expensive fabric that would be difficult to alter, you will not need to make muslins for most of your other projects. If you do lose or gain weight, have major surgery or a serious health crisis, or a number of years pass, we do recommend repeating the process of making a fitting pattern.

FITTING THROUGH THE YEARS

The passing of years is an especially important factor to consider. Even if you manage to control your weight and maintain good muscle tone through healthy diet and exercise, gravity cannot be staved off forever. Because of the natural shift of the internal organs over the years, even thin women discover that their abdomens eventually become relatively prominent and higher. Conversely, the buttocks tend to diminish with age; this change is especially noticeable in the way pants and narrow skirts fit. With the passage of time, the discs between the spinal vertebrae also compress and virtually everyone becomes shorter. This combination of the abdomen shift and the short-ened spine will affect the fitting of the bodice by significantly changing the distance between the base of the neck in front and the center of the waist curve. If the head and neck have also taken a more forward position and the shoulders have become rounded, additional fitting problems may emerge in the upper chest and back areas.

These are not changes you should be ashamed of or feel guilty about. They happen to everyone who lives to become what the Victorians graciously called a "woman of a certain age." Our experience is that many women who experienced relatively few concerns about fitting when they first began to sew can become increasingly frustrated with sewing after bearing children and, especially, after menopause. One of the

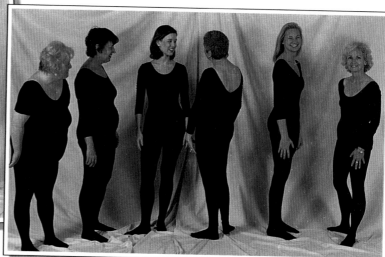

Bodies come in all shapes and sizes, and figure characteristics change through the years. Therefore, sewing patterns designed for an "average" figure can't possibly fit everyone perfectly.

secrets of achieving youthful appearance is recognizing what changes have occurred and employing the appropriate fitting and alteration techniques so that unsightly wrinkles or folds, stress points, and gaps do not call attention to aspects of your figure that you would rather disguise.

How is your courage holding up? For most of us, the next step is the most difficult of all—taking measurements. As mentioned earlier, one of the authors spent a number of years as a costume-maker for a youth ballet company. All young girls are self-conscious about their figures, especially as they begin to acquire womanly curves, and budding ballerinas can be especially so. Some of these girls spent up to 20 hours per week in leotards and

tights in front of highly critical teachers and unforgiving full-length mirrors. They were painfully aware of every bulge, even those that existed only in their imaginations!

The costume-maker finally resorted to taking their measurements in centimeters since, like most Americans, the dancers were relatively unfamiliar with the metric system and, therefore, less inclined to dispute the tape measure. If these young ladies, with what would seem to be virtually perfect figures, are so frightened of being measured, can we merely normal women be expected to remain calm?

As you and your fitting buddy begin this phase, keep in mind the goal: beautifully fitted garments that will make you look as if you shopped for them in the couture

houses of Paris, New York, London, and Milan. Be sure to keep your sense of humor and perspective close at hand. Your unique physical shape is the product of heredity and life experience even more than diet and exercise. Your shape does not define who you are. The clothes you put on come much closer to doing that, since they are a matter of choice and reflect your personal tastes and values. The fact that you are undertaking this process ensures that your clothes will fit you perfectly and will express the very best "you." A few minutes in a leotard or slip, in front of a friend armed with a harmless tape measure, are surely worth that goal. So, change your clothes, buck up your courage, and turn the page!

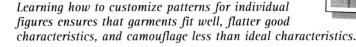

Learning how to customize patterns for individual figures ensures that garments fit well, flatter good characteristics, and camouflage less than ideal characteristics.

Chapter Three

Taking your measurements and preparing the fitting pattern

"I am tape-measure-phobic!"

—*Mother of three and grandmother of two*

Throughout the centuries, philosophers and theologians in many cultures and languages have agreed that the beginning of wisdom is self-knowledge. You are now embarking on a journey to self-knowledge. Congratulations!

Before beginning, you may wish to review the Basic Fitting Terms in Chapters One and Two. The directions and illustrations in this chapter will detail exactly how and where to take each measurement, so it is important to follow them carefully. It is also important that your tape measure be in good condition—free of folds or kinks, unstretched, and with no missing or illegible sections. If your tape measure has pronounced folds or kinks but is in otherwise good condition, try to flatten it with a barely warm dry iron and pressing cloth. If the

tape is made of plastic, be especially careful not to use more than the absolute minimum of heat.

It is vital that all measurements be taken in the correct place. The illustrations will help you do this, but you will also use strips of elastic at key spots on your body, to serve as visual cues. Cut one piece of elastic at least 4 inches (10 cm) larger than your waist, two others at least 4 inches (10 cm) larger than you think your bust measurement is, and another piece at least 6 inches (15 cm) bigger than you think your hips are at their widest point. Tie each of these around the appropriate area of your body, snug enough to stay in place but not so tightly as to cause distortion.

Other key points of reference when taking measurements are the neck point (N.P.), nape of the neck, shoulder point

Strips of elastic are tied at key reference points on the body: high bust, full bust, waist, and low hip.

(SH.P.), bust point (B.P.), and wrist bone. If you are wearing a long-sleeved leotard, your fitting buddy can mark these right on the leotard in chalk. You can also use stick-on dots and/or masking tape to mark these key areas. The masking tape is especially helpful since you can use the colored flow pen to mark the exact point.

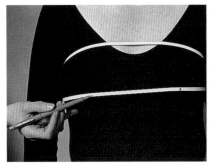

Marking the bust points on the elastic for reference.

As you take each measurement, remember that the goal is not to flatter yourself by achieving the smallest or largest possible number, but to make an accurate estimation of the actual circumference or length. The tape measure should be snug, not tight or loose.

Taking the high bust measurement.

Around the upper chest and bust, the tape measure should be close-fitting but cause no distortion. Around the waist, you should be able to feel the tape measure, but without a sensation of either tightness or looseness.

Around the fullest part of the hip, you should be able to hold the tape together at the appropriate number and easily move the tape up and down over the thighs, seat, and abdomen. To do this, you may need to loosen the tape a bit. The measured number may seem unusually large, especially in this last case, but remember that it is infinitely easier to remove extra width from pattern and fabric than it is to add width after cutting.

You will get more accurate measurements if you work with a fitting

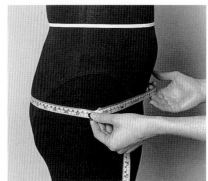

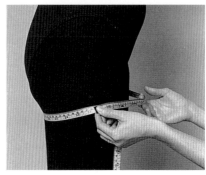

Taking the hip measurements, with tape measure held loosely enough to slide easily over the abdomen (top), seat (center), and thighs (bottom).

buddy. If you try to measure yourself, your twisting and bending to reach all the areas will distort the results.

Use the Personal Measurement Charts on pages 35-37 to record all measurements. You may wish to photocopy the charts so that you can use them more than once, especially if you sew for a number of people. It is a good idea to use a pencil to fill in the basic measurements, so that they can be revised, if needed.

NOTE: All measurements, whether on you or the pattern pieces, should be rounded up to the nearest $1/8$ inch (3 mm). More precise measurements are determined during and after fitting.

Note that the Personal Measurement Chart is organized from top down and the first column of blank spaces is for your measurements ("Body Measurements"). The next column ("Wearing Ease") indicates the preliminary amount of fitting ease, if any, for that specific area in a fitted dress. The next column ("Total Body Measurements") records your body measurements plus fitting ease, if appropriate. In the next column of blank spaces ("$1/2$-Total Body Measurements"), you will divide the circumference measurements in half, because the bodice and skirt **pattern pieces** are for only the right half of the garment. The next column ("Pattern Measurements") is where you indicate the actual measurements of the pattern pieces at each designated point. The pattern, of course, already includes the fitting ease. In the final blank column ("Changes"), you will calculate and record the amount of change you need to make in this area, so that the pattern pieces will equal your actual body measurements plus appropriate

fitting ease. During the tissue and muslin fittings, you may discover that you feel more comfortable with either more or less fitting ease than is suggested in the chart.

CIRCUMFERENCE MEASUREMENTS

The first measurements you will take are principally for determining the proper size pattern you should purchase. The key measurement for determining your correct pattern size does not even appear on the pattern envelope. It is the high bust measurement. As we mentioned earlier, this is because many women have busts that are either smaller or larger than a B cup. Obviously, these differences affect the bust measurement. However, a woman with a large bust does not necessarily have a broad back or wide shoulders, so she would have to make major back and shoulder adjustments to a pattern that was chosen for her actual bust measurement. A competitive swimmer, however, who may wear an A cup, typically would have broad shoulders, which would more likely be reflected in her high bust measurement than in her full bust measurement.

Measurements #1, #2, #3, and #4 are total circumference measurements. After they have been taken and recorded, your fitting buddy will pin a plumb line (see page 14 for making plumb line) at each armhole point and observe from the side

whether you tend to carry your weight to the front or to the back and if you have any unusual features such as a swayback or protruding abdomen, buttocks, or shoulder blades. Make notes of these observations on the Personal Measurement Chart, because these figure characteristics will affect the way a garment hangs.

Next, attach the plumb line to the high bust elastic at the armhole

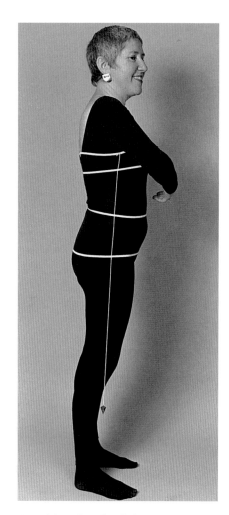

Attaching the plumb line, to determine figure characteristics of the front and back of the body.

Personal Measurement Chart – 1

	Body Measurements	Wearing Ease	Total Body Measurements	$\frac{1}{2}$-Total Body Measurements	Pattern Measurements	Changes + or –
	1. High Bust					
	2. Full Bust					
	2A. Bust Point Width	0"				
	2B. Front Bust	+1" (2.5 cm)				
	2C. Back Bust	+1" (2.5 cm)				
	3. Total Waist					
	3A. Front Waist	+$\frac{1}{2}$" (1.25 cm)				
	3B. Back Waist	+$\frac{1}{2}$" (1.25 cm)				

Record all measurements in the appropriate box, using a pencil in case revisions are needed later. You may wish to photocopy the charts so that you can use them more than once. NOTE: All body and pattern measurements should be rounded up to the nearest $\frac{1}{8}$ inch (3mm). The shaded boxes will not be filled in.

Personal Measurement Chart – 2

	Body Measurements	Wearing Ease	Total Body Measurements	¹/₂-Total Body Measurements	Pattern Measurements	Changes + or –
	4. Total Hip					
	4A. High Front Hip	+³/₄" (2 cm)				
	4B. Low Back Hip	+1" (2.5 cm)				
	5. Bicep	+2" (5 cm)				
	6A. Nape of Neck to Bust Point	0"				
	6B. Bust Point to Center Front	0"				

Name _____   Notes:

Date _____

Height _____ Weight _____

Size _____ Pattern Co. _____

Personal Measurement Chart – 3

	Body Measurements	Wearing Ease	Total Body Measurements	½-Total Body Measurements	Pattern Measurements	Changes + or –
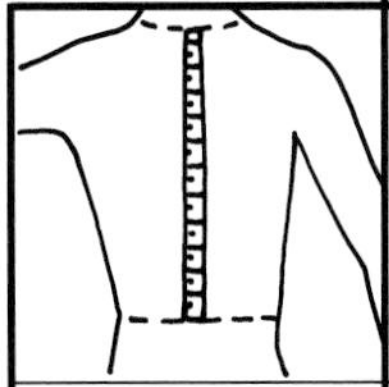	7. Center Back	0"				
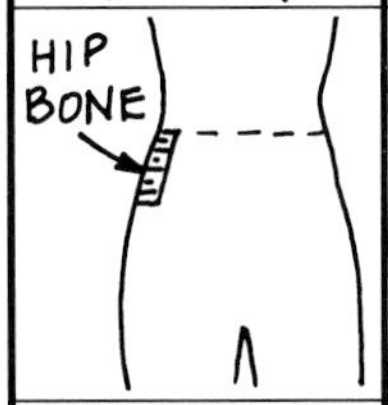	8A. Waistline to High Hipline	0"				
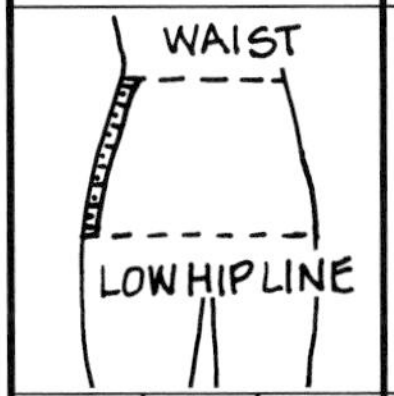	8B. Hip Depth _____	0"				
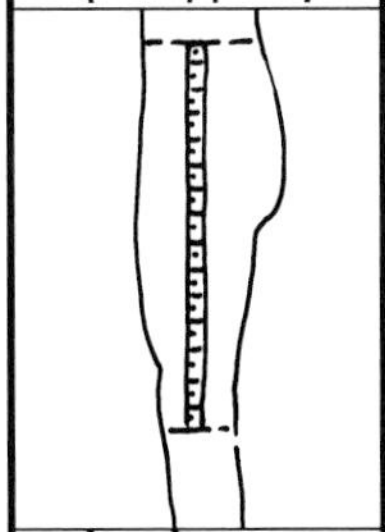	9. Waist to Knee	0"				
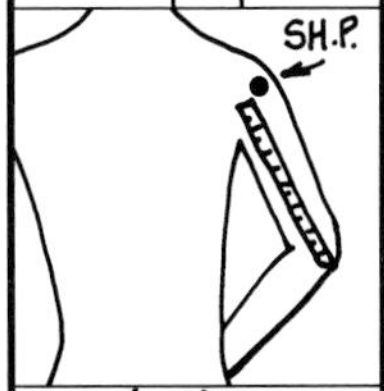	10. Shoulder to Elbow	0"				
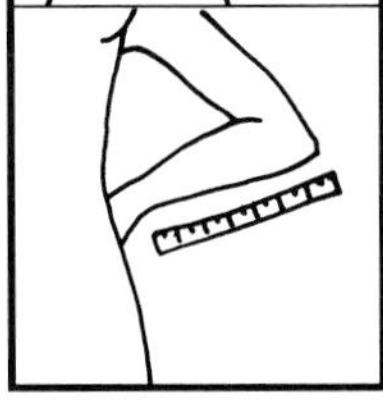	11. Elbow to Wrist	0"				

Name _____   Notes:

Date _____

Height _____ Weight _____

Size _____ Pattern Co. _____

37

point on each side, to determine the dividing points between your front and back at the high bust and full bust lines, the waist, and the high and low hiplines. These should be marked on the elastic. Since the patterns are divided from front to back, you must take the circumference measurements in the same way so that alterations can be made where they are actually needed.

The next measurement (#2A) is the distance between the right and left bust points. Measurement #2B is the total front bust measurement from side to side. Measurement #2C is across the back **at the bustline**, following the bustline elastic.

Measure the waistline (#3) next and remember that it is actually a curve. It is important that the tape measure follow this curve as it actually appears on your body, as indicated by the elastic. Take and record both the front waist (#3A) and back waist (#3B) measurements.

There are two sets of hip measurements—the high front hip and low back hip. The high hip (#4A) will be measured about 3 inches (7.5 cm) below the waistline at the fullest part of the abdomen. Here, you will take and record the high front hip measurement since this is the area where there are differences between various women and the pattern. These differences can be caused by a variety of factors, including an unusually flat stomach, protruding or high hip bones,

or a prominent abdomen.

Next you will measure and record the low back hip measurement (#4B). The low hip elastic in the back should be placed at the widest part of the **hip**, not at the thighs or below the crotch level. You will note that the sum of the high and low hip measurements (#4) is probably either smaller or larger than you thought your hips were. This is not peculiar to you—it would be impossible to capture both these areas in a single measurement. The result of measuring these areas separately is that now you know the actual maximum circumference of your body below the waist, as well as the exact areas in which any adjustment must be made.

The next measurement is the bicep (#5). This is taken just below the armhole point when your arm is relaxed. It corresponds, approximately, to the cap line on the pattern. The measurement should be taken with the arm slightly bent and the tape held close to the bicep but not so tightly as to cause distortion.

LENGTH MEASUREMENTS

The next measurements have to do with length. Remember that the pattern companies design for women who are 5 feet 6 inches (165 cm) tall. However, no two women this height have identical proportions. Some are relatively long-waisted or short-waisted; their legs and arms may be longer or

shorter than the so-called average, or their busts may be higher or lower than the pattern companies' standards. The following measurements are designed to pinpoint these individual differences so that you can adjust for them. Obviously, the millions of women who are taller or shorter than the "standard" height are going to have to make adjustments.

The first bodice length measurement (#6A) may seem unusual: from the nape of the neck to the bust point. The nape of the neck is generally considered to be the point where a jewel neckline would fall at the back, most usually at the prominent bone between the neck and the spine. This will help you determine if the bust point on your pattern needs to be raised (as it often does for very young figures) or lowered (as it does for most mature figures). The second measurement (#6B) is from the bust point down and across to the center front at the waistline. These two measurements identify whether the person is short- or long-waisted and also precisely where the length needs to be adjusted—above or below the bust point, or in both areas.

The final bodice length measurement is the center back (#7), from the nape of the neck to the waistline. Women with rounded upper backs, unusually developed back muscles, or protruding shoulder blades will require additional length as well as width in the middle and upper back.

The next two measurements are just for your reference, to determine the general shape of the hip curve: the distance from the waistline to the top of the hip bone or the high hip curve (#8A) and to the fullest part of the hip or hip depth (#8B). Pattern companies have placed the high hip at 3 to $3^1/2$ inches (7.5 to 9 cm) below the waist on the side seam and the hip depth at $8^1/2$ to 9 inches (21.5 to 23 cm) below the waist. It is important to note whether your figure significantly differs; this observation will enable you to choose the proper hip curve should you have to redraw the stitching line and, therefore, the cutting line for the skirt and pants patterns. These two measurements become important when you are working with the pants fitting pattern in Chapter Eight.

Also for reference, you will measure the length from your waist at the side waist point to the middle of your knee (#9). Fashion patterns often will indicate the finished length of the skirt, and even if you do not usually make a skirt length adjustment, you might wish to do so if the designer has decreed a length significantly shorter or longer than you feel comfortable wearing. You may also cut the tissue pattern to this length to save muslin, since no hem allowance will be needed for the muslin fitting, but be sure to add

a hem allowance back when using your fitting pattern to create or alter a real garment.

The next two measurements are related to sleeve length and are based on the lengths generally recommended for dresses—to the bottom of the wrist bone. Jackets are often slightly shorter, to expose a bit of "linen" if worn over a shirt or long-sleeved blouse, and coats are slightly longer, to completely cover both jacket and blouse or shirt. Since these variations in length are built into the patterns, like the greater fitting ease requirements in jackets and coats, you can expect to make the same basic modifications to them as you do to your dress sleeve pattern.

The first sleeve measurement (#10) is from the shoulder point to the elbow. Your elbow should be slightly bent, arm held slightly forward and raised to waist level; measure from the shoulder point to the elbow. The second measurement (#11) is taken with the arm in the same slightly raised, forward, and bent position, from the elbow to the bottom of the wrist bone.

CHOOSING YOUR FITTING PATTERN

You now have all the personal measurements you will need to complete your basic dress pattern. Later on, you will take a few additional measurements for the pants pattern. In the Total Fit classes at

G Street Fabrics, we have discovered that shoulder length, chest, and armhole measurements are not needed at this point because these areas are best adjusted after observation during the tissue and muslin fittings.

After you have assessed your figure by studying yourself in a full-length mirror, considered the input of your fitting buddy, and taken your measurements as detailed above, you are ready to select a brand and size of fitting pattern.

When choosing the correct size for you, remember that the number on the envelope will have little or no relation to the size you generally purchase in ready-to-wear. The size will be known only to you and to the sales assistant in the pattern department of your favorite store, for the few seconds it takes her to ring up your pattern. Regardless of that number on the envelope, choose the size to which you will have to make the fewest and least drastic changes. Generally, the key measurement is your high bust or upper chest, since this affects both the shape and placement of the armholes and the width of the chest, shoulders, and neck—some of the most difficult areas to adjust.

The rule of thumb is that, if your bust measurement differs by 2 inches (5 cm) or less from your high bust measurement, you should choose your pattern size for a fitted dress according to your bust mea-

surement. If the difference is greater
than 2 inches (5 cm), you should
choose the pattern size according to
your high bust measurement. Waist
and hip changes to the dress are
easier to make than upper chest,
upper back, neck, and shoulder
changes. If you are making a skirt
or pants, however, the hip measurement is more significant. The goal is
to avoid making any adjustment of
more than 4 inches (10 cm). This
reduces the chance of distortion and
also preserves the original lines of
the garment.

PREPARING THE PATTERN

Once you have chosen the pattern
brand and size best suited to your
figure and your fashion tastes, careful preparation of the tissue assures
the greatest accuracy in the personal
fitting pattern you will ultimately
develop. If your pattern is multi-
sized, as the Style and Burda patterns are, use a fine-tip colored flow
pen to trace the size you will be
cutting. If you are one size for the
bust (again, as determined by your
high bust measurement if you wear
other than a B cup), another size for
the waist, and yet another for the
hip, trace the armhole, shoulder, and
neck for the bust size. Next, choose
the appropriate lines for your waist
and hip, and blend the lines
between sizes as you move with
your flow pen from one area to the
other. See Figure 1.

If there is only one cutting line

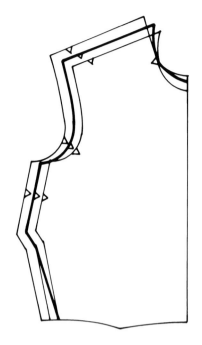

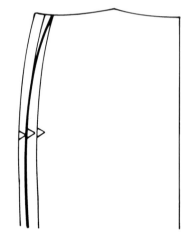

*Figure 1. Marking the appropriate
cutting line on a multi-size pattern.*

for all the sizes on a multi-size pattern, but different stitching lines for
each size, use the colored pen to
mark the appropriate stitching line
for your size. Simplicity and
McCall's include extra tissue
between the lengthen/shorten lines

to use if you must make the pattern
longer. At the outset, you should
fold these lines together and secure
them with tape. The Vogue and
Butterick patterns indicate three
shoulder points; choose the middle
one for fitting and alterations.

Then, rough-cut your pattern,
allowing the greatest amount of
extra tissue possible above the
sleeve cap and, in particular, along
side seams. The next step may seem
somewhat obsessive/compulsive to
some of you: use a warm dry iron
and pressing cloth to carefully iron
each piece, removing all fold lines
and wrinkles. This step is necessary
because the machines that prepare
patterns for the envelope are anything but gentle, and the wrinkles
can make a pattern significantly
smaller than the pattern-maker
intended. This is also a good time to
iron the extra tissue paper so that it
is wrinkle-free. NOTE: If you cannot
store your pattern pieces flat, roll
them onto a cardboard tube for
storage. This will save you from
having to re-iron them each time
you need them.

Once you have completed these
preliminary steps, you are ready to
measure the key areas on the pattern and begin calculating and then
making adjustments. We usually
recommend that you leave the pattern in the rough-cut stage, retaining as much tissue as possible on
the edges to allow for adjustments
you may need to make. Using the

fine tip pen and measuring carefully with the flexible ruler, draw a dashed line (if one is not already provided) to represent the stitching line 5/8 inch (16 mm) inside the original cutting line as provided by the manufacturer. When the seamline passes through a dart, do not draw anything between the two legs of the dart; this omission will make measuring the finished dimensions of waistline, high hipline, and bustline much easier. See Figure 2.

With the same pen, add the fol-

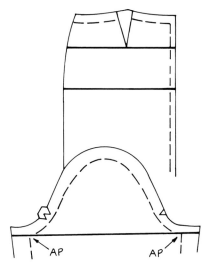

Figure 2. Drawing in the bustline and stitching line, skipping over darts.

lowing if they are not already included on your pattern: bust point, bustline, hipline (a horizontal line just below the darts), low back hipline (at the widest point of the seat curve), and sleeve cap line (a horizontal line connecting the arm-

hole points on each side of the sleeve). See Figures 2 and 3.

Figure 3. Drawing in the high hipline in the front and the low hipline in the back, and the sleeve cap line.

MEASURING THE PATTERN

You will need to measure your selected pattern at each of the points you measured on yourself. When you do this, remember to measure along the line provided, eliminating the seam allowances and skipping over darts. Since many of these measurements actually are along curved lines, this is a good time to learn to work with the flexible ruler. Turn it on its edge along the curved **seamline** and measure the total distance, excluding any darts, between seamlines. These numbers should be recorded in the "Pattern Measurements" column on the Personal Measurement Chart. Because the **pattern pieces**

cover only one quarter of the body, their measurements will correspond with the numbers you have recorded in the "1/2-Total Body Measurements" column.

In the final "Changes" column, calculate the amount of correction (+ or -) you will need to make in that particular area of the pattern by comparing your 1/2-total body measurements to those of the pattern. In the following chapters we will walk you, step by step, through these corrections.

Now you can put on your robe or slip into some comfortable clothes that you can easily remove when it comes time to pin-fit the pattern tissue. Relax—the worst is over. You and your fitting buddy have certainly earned another cup of tea or glass of lemonade. Now you know yourself, so you have taken the first steps toward wisdom—and toward the beautifully fitted clothes you have always desired.

The flexible ruler, turned on its edge, is used to measure curved lines.

Chapter Four

Fitting problems and solutions

Many of the staff members of G Street Fabrics helped us prepare for this book by attending what we called "Misfit Sunday." They brought in garments they made straight from the pattern envelope, but do not wear because of a variety of fitting problems. In the "before" photographs, you can see some of these and other problem garments modeled by the women who made them. You will notice that poorly-fitting garments don't look comfortable to wear, don't hang correctly, and are not very flattering to the figure.

By following the simple alteration techniques explained in this book, the women re-made the same patterns to achieve the better-fitting and figure-flattering garments in the "after" photographs.

Elizabeth has always avoided wearing straight skirts because they generally don't have enough width across the thighs if they fit her small waist, resulting in unattractive folds and wrinkles across the front, as in the skirt at left. To solve this, she cuts a multi-size pattern along different lines to accommodate her waist, hip, and thigh measurements. In the skirt at right, she gets a good fit at the waist and extra width at the level of the thighs, for a smooth, flattering look.

At left, Nancy can hardly move in this jacket that is too narrow around the bust and hip, but too wide in the shoulder/chest area. She made a number of adjustments at right: L-slash correction to reduce chest/shoulder width in back and front, exterior corrections to add bust and hip circumference, addition of bust dart, addition to sleeve cap height, and L-slash alteration to move armhole for greater range of motion.

At left, Chris's jacket reveals a combination of fitting flaws: too much fabric at the shoulders and a too-short sleeve cap, which pulls the shoulder down. Additionally, the jacket front separates because there is not enough width at the sides and in the bust area. At right, her jacket front and sleeves hang better, as a result of a bust cup correction, added width at sides and sleeve bicep, added height to sleeve cap, and an L-slash correction to reduce width at the shoulders.

At left, Nancy's pants are too tight in the crotch and around the waist and hips, so that they are unflattering and uncomfortable to wear. At right, the altered pattern fits her properly and illustrates how perfect fit can actually camouflage figure challenges. She re-curved the back crotch seam and added length to the back crotch at the waist. She also added circumference to the waist and hips, using an interior correction because the pant design has no side seams. The finished pants are flattering and slimming.

At left, Joy's tunic and skirt ensemble looks too big and baggy for her, but the sleeves are too short. For the better-fitting version at right, she lowered the back waistline of the skirt so it hangs straight. She also used an L-slash alteration to reduce width in the shoulder/chest area, lengthened the sleeves, moved the front waist darts under the bust points, and added a bit of circumference at the hip.

The blouse at left fits Andrea the way she likes it, except that the sleeves are too long, even when the cuff is buttoned. By simply shortening the sleeves at the lengthen/shorten lines on the pattern, the blouse at right fits her better and the cuff stays put at the wrist.

Left, Mary's jacket fits tightly around her waist and hips, and has too much width in the shoulder/chest area. To make her jacket fit better, at right, she made the bust cup correction, added a side bust dart, added circumference at the waist and high hip, and reduced width in the shoulder/chest area with an L-slash alteration. Now her jacket buttons comfortably in front, fits her better at the shoulder and bustline, and hangs evenly all the way around.

Left, Marietta's jacket doesn't have enough fabric to comfortably cover her long curved back, so it pulls at the back waist and wrinkles across her upper back. At right, her altered jacket hangs smoothly due to the prominent curve alteration she made to add length and width in the back. She also made a bust cup correction to this princess style jacket, to fit her generous front curves without adding extra fabric at the chest and shoulder.

Farideh made the same pattern for two very different looks. However, at left, the neckline is too large for her petite figure and excess fabric in the shoulder/chest area causes wrinkles at the shoulders and droopy sleeves. At right, she redrew a smaller neckline and made an L-slash correction to reduce width in the shoulder/chest area.

Marisa's pants at left are too tight across the seat and hips, resulting in unattractive folds and gapping at the top of the zipper. The plaid fabric also emphasizes the width of her figure. To achieve the more flattering look at right, she chose a solid color and altered the front and back crotch curves, and made an external correction to the side seams at the hipline. Because she likes to wear pants low on the hip, she also lowered the entire waistline and the curve of the front waist.

At left, Gard's pants are too tight in the back crotch and at the side seams, causing excess bagginess at the back of the leg and gapping at the pocket. She re-curved the back crotch, added to the crotch point, and made slight exterior corrections to the side seams for the sleek fit at right.

Tracy buys size 4 patterns to fit her petite figure. However, when she makes them right out of the pattern envelope, they are still too large all over, like the dress at left. To down-size the pattern for the better-fitting dress at right, she has to use an interior correction to reduce width all over, use the lengthen/shorten lines to reduce length all over, and then raise the armhole point.

At left, Dottie's princess style dress is too long at the shoulder seam and too tight at the bust, waist, and hip. These fitting problems, combined with the bold printed fabric, actually emphasize her weight. After making just a few alterations, the dress fits better and has a slimming effect. Dottie made the princess style bust cup correction to add circumference, external corrections to the princess front and side front pieces for additional circumference at the waist and hip, and a slash and pivot correction to reduce the shoulder seam without affecting chest width.

Chapter Five

Fitting the bodice

"I used to be high-busted, but gravity and three children took care of that! Now I have the opposite problem."

—Nancy, G Street Fabrics sewing specialist and teacher

Did you ever take elementary physics? If so, you may recall that "For every action, there is a reaction." The same holds true in pattern-fitting: every change you make affects another part of the pattern. Your goal is to make necessary changes while preserving the original lines of the design and end up with a pattern that still lies flat.

In this and other chapters, we will designate adjustments as major or minor and consider them in the order in which they must be made on a specific area of the garment. All major adjustments in pattern-fitting, especially in the bodice, involve prominent curves or simultaneously affect two or more areas of the pattern with a single adjustment. For prominent curves, the basic principle is: **the greater the three-dimensional curve, the more length and width you will have to add to the pattern.** (A three-dimensional curve has height or depth as well as length and width.) The opposite is also true: for less prominent curves, both length and width will need to be subtracted.

This rule comes into special play in the bodice, because all pattern companies create patterns for a B cup size. If you wear an A cup or, especially, if you wear a C cup or larger, you will encounter fitting problems and will have to perform a major bust cup correction. Other bodice areas that often require major alterations are the shoulder and front chest area or across the back and the upper back.

MAJOR ADJUSTMENTS TO BODICE FRONT

The bust cup correction can be easily anticipated, based on the bra cup size you wear; this should be the first correction you make on the pattern tissue. Shoulder and front chest and upper back adjustments are best made after the tissue fit, because you will get a clearer idea of exactly what kind, location, and amount of correction is needed when you model the pattern. You will begin bodice corrections in the front, because these corrections affect all others.

BUST CUP ADJUSTMENT

The bust cup correction, if necessary, is the first alteration to be made. It is designed to add both width and length to the exact area in which it is needed. The

Basic Fitting Terms

Review the following terms from Chapter One: ALTERATION LINE, BLENDING or TRUEING, BODICE, BUST POINT, CROSS-WISE GRAIN, DART, FASHION RULER™, FLEXIBLE RULER, FRENCH CURVE RULER, GRAINLINE, GUIDELINE, HINGE, HORIZON-TAL, LENGTHWISE GRAIN, PIVOT POINT, SEAM ALLOWANCE, SELVAGE, SLASH, SQUARE A LINE, and VERTICAL. Review from Chapter Two: ARMHOLE POINT, ARM-SCYE, BUST DARTS, CAP LINE, CAP OF SLEEVE, CENTER LINE, CIRCUMFERENCE, EASE ALLOWANCE, FITTING EASE, NECK POINT, SEAMLINE, SHOULDER POINT, SIDE WAIST POINT, and WAIST DARTS.

CLOSURES. Seamlines to be left unsewn for insertion of zipper, buttons and button-holes, or hooks and eyes. Buttons with buttonholes and zippers with plackets involve some overlapping, while the two sides of the seam may be merely adjacent if they are to be joined by hooks and eyes or buttons and loops. If there is to be an overlap, it is especially important to note where the center line of each piece is marked. The Vogue and Butterick fitting patterns are designed for front closures, but we think you can get a truer idea of correct fit with a back closure. In fact, since this is not a garment that is designed to be worn, it is best not to insert a zipper or any other formal closure.

DART LEGS. The two broken lines on a pattern that meet at the dart point or end and indicate the stitching line that will join the two sides of the dart.

DART MID-LINE. A guideline for pattern-making and alteration that runs through the midpoint of the dart base to the dart point; it becomes a fold line when the dart is closed or a slash line for some alterations.

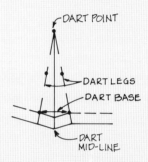

DART POINT or END. The point where the dart legs converge; often used as a hinge or pivot point when making alterations.

DART WIDTH or BASE. The distance between the two dart legs at the stitching line at the base of the dart. The wider the dart base, the greater the three-dimensional curve becomes.

DRAPING. The pattern-making technique whereby a flat piece of cloth is laid over the figure or dress form and shaped by the addition of darts or seams.

most common correction is the enlargement of this area for a C cup figure or greater. There may be some individuals who need to reduce it for an A cup or smaller; the basic technique is the same, but to reduce the bust curve, length and width are decreased by overlapping tissue, rather than increasing both dimensions by spreading the cut edges apart.

As mentioned earlier, if your bustline measurement is 2 inches (5 cm) larger than your high bust, you probably wear a B cup and need no adjustment. Figures with less than $1^{1}/_{2}$ inches (4 cm) difference wear an A cup or smaller and usually can wear the B cup bodice without adjustment. If you find, however, that bodices usually have vertical folds over your bust area, you may wish to take out some of the fullness. Women who wear a C cup or larger, however, will definitely benefit from the bust cup correction. Not only will binding across the bust be eliminated, but the side seam, armhole, and even the neckline will fit more smoothly without gaps or stress wrinkles.

To determine how much correction must be made, compare your full bust and high bust measurements. For a C cup, there is usually 3 inches (7.5 cm) difference between the full bust and high bust; this is 1 inch (2.5 cm) more than would be found on a B cup figure. The bust cup correction rule of thumb is: the difference between the full bust and high bust measurements, minus the B cup allowance of 2 inches (5 cm), divided by 2 equals the amount of correction needed

to the front pattern piece. The following is an example of this rule in action:

Full bust measurement	37 inches (94 cm)
Minus high bust measurement	34 inches (86.5 cm)
Difference	3 inches (7.5 cm)
Minus B cup allowance	2 inches (5 cm)
Total correction required to front	1 inch (2.5 cm)
One half of total correction per pattern piece	$^{1}/_{2}$ inch (1.25 cm)

Therefore, if the difference between your high bust and full bust is 3 inches (7.5 cm), you will add $^{1}/_{2}$ inch (1.25 cm) more in width to the bustline area on each side of the bodice front and approximately the same amount in length by doing the bust cup correction.

If, after applying this formula, you discover that you need to make a total correction of more than 1 inch (2.5 cm), you wear larger than a D cup. In this case, you will need to perform both of the bust cup corrections outlined below: Method One to add the first 1 inch (2.5 cm) in width and some of the extra length you require, and Method Two to provide any additional correction needed.

If you try to make the entire D cup correction with Method One alone, you will discover that the darts will be too pointy and the armhole seam will become extremely distorted. On the other hand, if you use Method Two alone, you will not get the additional length you need, and you may add width to the chest area that you do not require. If you still require more correction after following both methods, make it at the side seams.

Bust Cup Correction: Method One

This method adds up to a total of 2 inches (5 cm) additional width to the entire front bodice, and approximately 1 inch (2.5 cm) in length to the bust area—without affecting the upper chest or shoulder. It does cause some armhole distortion, however, which is why it should be used to make only up to 1 inch (2.5 cm) correction for the front pattern piece. Perform the correction following these steps:

1. Extend the mid-line of the waist dart up to the center of the bust point symbol. If no symbol has been provided, extend the mid-lines of the bust dart and waist dart until they converge—this is the bust point.

2. Draw a dot on the armhole seamline opposite the single notch.

3. Clip through the seam allowance to, but not through, the dot.

4. Draw a second line at an angle from the bust point up to the dot.

5. Draw a third line through the center of the bust dart to the bust point. See Figure 1.

6. Slash through the center of the waist dart to the bust point and then at an angle out to, but not through, the dot you made on the armhole seam, creating a hinge at the seamline.

7. Cut through the center of the bust dart up to meet the other slashes at the bust point, creating another hinge there.

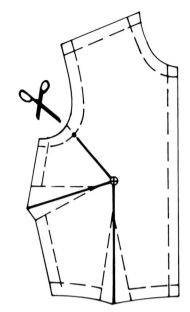

Figure 1. Slash lines for bust cup correction.

8. Carefully place the pattern over extra tissue on the cork or foam core mat.

9. Pin along the inside edge of the waist dart slash and the slash to the armhole up to the hinge; place a pin through the hinge.

10. Gently pull the rest of the pattern down and out, spreading open a rectangle along the waist dart slash. This rectangle should be $1/2$ inch (1.25 cm) wide for a C cup, and can be up to 1 inch (2.5 cm) for larger sizes to compensate for the extra difference between your high bust and full bust measurements. If you need more, make the maximum correction possible using this method, and then use Method Two to gain additional width. Pin and then tape securely in place.

11. As you gently pull on the lower outside portion of the pattern, a triangular shaped insertion will open at the bust dart and another along the slash to the armhole. See Figure 2. You will notice that the tissue along the clip you made in the armhole seam allowance will overlap so that the pattern lies flat; pin this section in place, to keep it flat while taping.

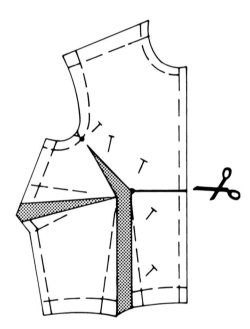

Figure 2. Bust cup correction with slash line for lengthening center front.

12. Use removable tape to hold everything in place. Tape all slashes firmly because, in the tissue-fitting phase, untaped portions will create pesky bulges.

13. Since the bodice is now uneven at the hem, you must lengthen the center front to match the side front at the waistline. Draw a horizontal line from the bust point through the center front seam allowance. See Figure 2.

14. Slash along this line and, over tissue, slide the lower center front down until it lines up at the waistline. Pin and then tape in place. See Figure 3.

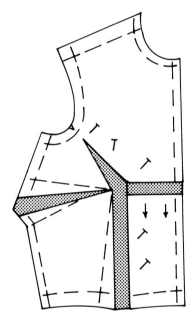

Figure 3. Bust cup and front waistline correction.

Bust Cup Correction: Method Two

This correction adds up to another 1 inch (2.5 cm) of width to the front pattern piece beyond the previous method. It is recommended for those who wear a double D cup or larger and who need still more width than the previous method can provide. This alteration also provides more width to the upper chest

area without adding to the shoulder. Furthermore, it does not significantly alter the armhole shape or length of the pattern. Perform this correction, following these steps:

1. Extend the mid-line of the new waist dart to the shoulder seamline; make a dot where the line meets the shoulder seamline.

2. Clip through the shoulder seam allowance at the dot, to create a hinge.

3. Extend the mid-line of the bust dart to the bust point or until it intersects the waist dart mid-line. See Figure 4.

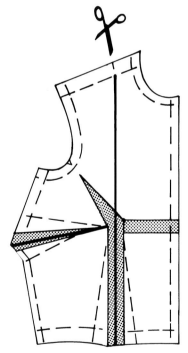

Figure 4. Slash lines for additional front width.

4. Slash through the center of the waist dart up to, but not through,

the dot on the shoulder seamline.

5. Slash through the center of the bust dart to, but not through, the bust point or extended waist dart mid-line.

6. Choose a second color of tissue to distinguish this correction from the Method One correction and carefully place the pattern over the new tissue on the cork or foam core mat.

7. Pin along the inside edge of the waist dart slash and through the hinge at the shoulder seamline.

8. Gently pull the pattern out, spreading open another rectangle along the waist dart. See Figure 5. Continue opening the rectangle until

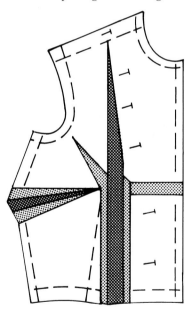

Figure 5. Front bodice corrected for bust cup and additional width.

its width equals the amount you need to add, up to an additional 1 inch (2.5 cm). Tape securely in place.

9. This correction will result in a triangular insertion in the chest area above the bust line, but with no bulge at the shoulder line. It has also added width in the chest area and spread the bust dart open a bit more. If you still need additional width, add it at the side seams.

Once you have reached this point, you and your fitting buddy have earned a mutual pat on the back! You have just made one of the most complex adjustments in pattern-fitting. The basic principles underlying

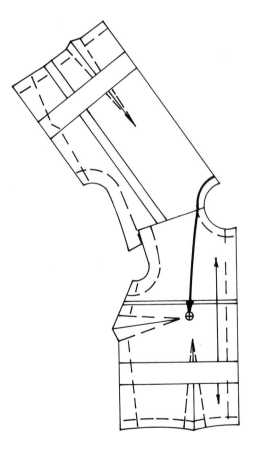

Figure 6. Overlapping front and back bodice pieces to re-measure distance from nape of neck to bust point (measurement #6A).

what you have done so far are what pattern-fitting and pattern-making are all about: (1) three-dimensional curves require both greater length and width of fabric than do flat surfaces, and (2) every action creates a reaction. It really is not all that mysterious, is it?

BUST POINT AND DART CORRECTIONS

These corrections should be done first if you do not require the bust cup correction. If you have made a bust cup correction, these should be the next adjustments you make. Whether or not you have made the bust cup change, you must check to be certain that the bust point on the pattern is in the correct position.

To do this, lay the front and back bodice pattern pieces on a table with the shoulder seamlines overlapping; match the neck points. Using the flexible ruler on its edge, measure from the center back at the neck seamline around the neck point (where shoulder seamlines meet the neck seamline) and down to the bust point. See Figure 6. Compare this measurement to what you recorded on the Personal Measurement Chart (#6A) and make a mark on the pattern at the correct level. Then, consult Measurement #2A on the chart and, at the bust point level you have indicated on the pattern, measure in this distance from the center front and redraw the bust point symbol. Once you

have determined the correct position of the bust point on the pattern, make sure that both darts are pointing to the bust point. If not, one or both darts may need to be moved.

Moving bust and waist darts

The easiest way to move darts is to use the box method, following these steps:

1. If it is not already indicated, draw the mid-line of the dart(s) to be moved. Note that the waist dart may now have a big rectangle of new tissue in the middle of it because of a bust cup correction. If this is the case, draw the line vertically through the middle of the new tissue, parallel to the grainline or center front.

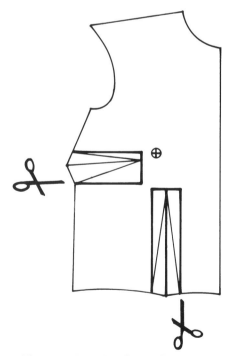

Figure 7. Drawing boxes for moving darts.

2. Draw two more lines exactly parallel to the first; each line runs through the point where a dart leg intersects the seamline

3. Square a line through the dart point that connects the three lines you drew in steps 1 and 2 and forms a box around the dart. See Figure 7.

4. Cut out the box along the outer lines and move the entire dart to its new location, adding tissue as needed. The waist dart point should be directly below the bust point; the bust dart point should be opposite the bust point. See Figure 8.

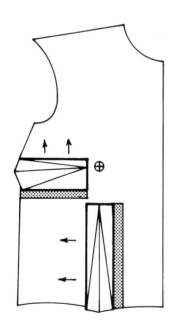

Figure 8. Moving bust and waist darts.

Redrawing the darts

After moving darts, the ends of the darts may need to be redrawn. You can do this now or wait until after making any other needed changes to the bodice front. To redraw the darts, follow these steps:

1. Extend the mid-line of the waist dart to the bust point and mark a new dart point 1 inch (2.5 cm) below the bust point. Extend the mid-line of the bust dart to the bust point and mark a new dart point 1 to 1½ inches (2.5 to 4 cm) away from the bust point. NOTE: You may have to adjust these new

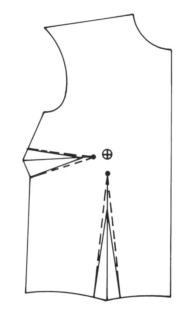

Figure 9. Redrawing darts after moving.

dart points again during the tissue and/or muslin fittings.

2. Redraw the dart legs. See Figure 9. For the bust dart, the legs should intersect the side seamline at the original points. If you have made a bust cup correction, this dart will have become either deeper or narrower. For the waist dart, the legs should intersect with the original points on the waistline. This

dart may also have become either wider or narrower as a result of a bust cup correction. If the waist dart base is too wide, it may cause stress lines; if so, the dart base can be reduced to add circumference at the front waist.

MINOR ADJUSTMENTS TO BODICE FRONT

Minor adjustments can be made either by adding to or subtracting from the side seams or adjusting the length along the lengthen/shorten lines provided on the pattern.

LENGTHENING OR SHORTENING THE BODICE FRONT

Measure the front bodice pattern from the bust point to the center front of the waist and compare to Measurement #6B on the Personal Measurement Chart; any bust cup corrections you have made have probably affected this measurement. Measure the back bodice pattern from nape of neck to the center back waistline and compare to Measurement #7 on the Personal Measurement Chart. Lengthen or shorten the front and back pattern pieces equally. If you need to lengthen or shorten different amounts to the front and back, choose the smaller correction for both pieces. Further corrections will be determined and made during the tissue fit. Use the lengthen/shorten lines provided on the pattern to lengthen by slashing and spreading, or to shorten by slashing and overlapping or folding an even tuck. Review page 15 in Chapter One for a detailed description of this technique. Blend seamlines and redraw darts as needed.

ADJUSTING CIRCUMFERENCE AT THE SIDE SEAMS

As a general rule, try not to make additions to or subtractions from the side seams of more than 1 inch (2.5 cm) per pattern piece, for a total of 4 inches (10 cm) total circumference. Larger changes will result in distortion of the basic design and placement of darts and other shaping devices.

The one exception to this general 1-inch (2.5-cm) rule is that, if you have changed either the bust or the waist at the side seam of the bodice, you may add 1 inch (2.5 cm) to the other plus the amount you have already added to the first area. This exception also applies to waist/hip changes. For example, if you have added $1/2$ inch (1.25 cm) to the side seam at the bustline, you may add up to $1^1/2$ inches (4 cm) to the same seam at the waist. If you have added 1 inch (2.5 cm) to the waist at the side seam of the skirt, you may add up to 2 inches (5 cm) to the hips. See Figure 10. If you have taken in the bust, however, by $1/2$ inch (1.25 cm), you may only add $1/2$ inch (1.25 cm) at the waist. Sometimes, if only a slight difference is needed, the change can be

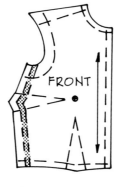

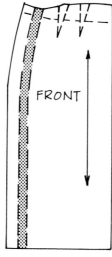

Figure 10. Adding circumference at side seams.

accommodated by slight additions to or subtractions from the darts, up to a maximum of $1/2$ inch (1.25 cm) on each side of the dart legs at the base. Every change you make, rounded up to the nearest $1/8$ inch (3 mm), must be recorded so that you will remember to make it on all the patterns you use.

With this general rule in mind, re-measure the front bust circumference of the pattern and compare it to your personal front bust measurement (#2B). Do the same for the front waist of the pattern, compar-

ing it with your personal front waist measurement (#3A). Once you have determined the amount of change needed at the side seams, use the flexible ruler to measure and mark the exact amount of addition or subtraction needed at the waist point and full bust.

Redrawing the Side Seam and Darts after Circumference Adjustments

After making circumference adjustments, the bust and waist darts will need to be temporarily folded closed and redrawn along with the side seamline. Do not attempt to redraw the side seam of the front without closing the bust dart, following these steps:

1. Fold a crease out toward you along the lower leg of the bust dart.

2. At the dart point, fold the bodice front area to the underside; do not crease the pattern.

3. Place the pattern onto the cork or foam core mat and place a pin at the dart point to act as a hinge.

4. Bring the lower creased dart leg up to meet the uncreased upper leg.

5. Fold in place and tape closed temporarily.

6. Draw a straight seamline from the new armhole point to the new side waist point.

7. Place the 1-inch (2.5-cm) line of the ruler's grid along the new seamline and redraw a new cutting line 1 inch (2.5 cm) beyond the new seamline.

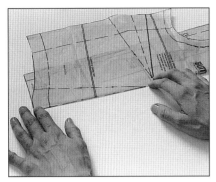 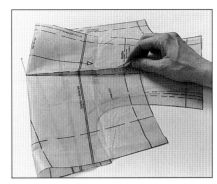 

After making circumference adjustments, darts must be temporarily closed, in order to accurately redraw seamlines. The dart leg nearest the center is creased, the upper bodice folded under at the dart point, the pattern pinned to the cork board through the dart point, and the creased leg brought over to meet the other leg.

8. While the dart is closed, cut away the extra tissue along the new cutting line.

9. Untape the dart and note the new shape of the dart base.

If the waist dart was used to adjust waist circumference or was affected by the bust cup correction, the shape of the dart base will need to be corrected. Folding the waist dart closed is similar to the procedure for the bust dart. Follow these steps:

1. Fold a crease out toward you along the dart leg closest to the center front. See photo above, left.

2. Fold the upper bodice to the underside at the waist dart point. See photo above, center.

3. Place the pattern and pin the dart point onto the cork or foam core mat.

4. Bring the creased dart leg over to the uncreased outer leg.

5. Tape or pin the dart closed temporarily. See photo above, right.

6. Blend the curve of the waistline seam, as necessary.

7. Add a 1-inch (2.5-cm) seam allowance.

8. Cut away the extra tissue along the cutting line.

9. Untape the dart and note the new shape of the dart base.

Major Adjustments to Bodice Back

Relax—these alterations are usually much less complicated than those for the front. The most complex is the correction for a prominent curve in the upper back, which is technically similar to the bust cup adjustment. You and your fitting buddy have already noted if this is a problem while you were doing your figure assessment. If so, it will most likely require a major alteration. You may wish to postpone it until after the tissue fit, to be sure that it is really necessary and to determine a more accurate measurement.

Adjusting for a Prominent Back Curve

A less common fitting problem area than the bust is the upper back. The combination of varying shoulder slopes, differences in muscle development, spinal curvatures, shoulder blade characteristics, and bone structure, when combined with the greater need for fitting ease in this hard-working part of the body, can present its own challenge for alteration. Almost no one matches the statistical average for which commercial patterns are designed. To make this adjustment, follow these steps:

1. Draw a horizontal line across the upper back, from the center back through the shoulder dart point and to the shoulder point. If you are using the McCall's fitting pattern, you will notice that this line is already provided.

2. Draw a second line through the middle of the shoulder dart. If there

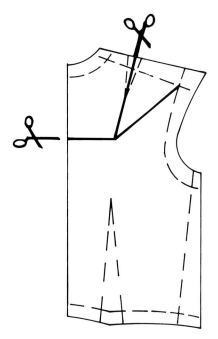

Figure 11. Slash lines for prominent back curve alteration.

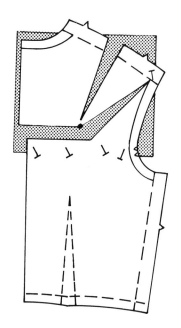

Figure 12. Finished alteration for prominent upper back curve.

is no dart, draw a slightly angled line down from the middle of the shoulder to the horizontal line. See Figure 11.

3. Slash along the horizontal line to, but not through, the shoulder point; clip the seam allowance to create a hinge at this point.

4. Slash along the dart or diagonal line to, but not through, the horizontal line, to create a hinge at this point.

5. Carefully place the pattern over tissue on the cork or foam core mat.

6. Pin along the lower edge of the horizontal slash and at the shoulder hinge.

7. Spread the pattern up. A rectangle will form above the horizontal slash, from 1/2 to 1 inch (1.25 to 2.5 cm) wide; the shoulder dart will

open wider or, if there was no shoulder dart, a new one will form. See Figure 12. NOTE: This extra width can be eased into the shoulder seam if you do not want to create a dart.

8. Pin and then tape the alteration securely in place.

9. Blend all seamlines and cutting lines, and redraw darts if necessary. The center back seamline or fold line should be extended down to remain a straight line.

Minor Adjustments to Bodice Back
Lengthening or Shortening the Bodice Back

To keep the front side seam and back side seam the same length, use either the front measurement as a

guide or divide the difference between the two in half, then add to one and subtract from the other. If you have made the prominent back curve alteration, lengthen or shorten the lower back to coordinate the front and back side seams.

Fitting patterns offer two options for lengthening and shortening the back bodice. Any correction at the upper lengthen/shorten line, which runs into the armhole, would make the armhole bigger or smaller and require redrawing the armhole. Therefore, use only the lower set of lines to make the needed length correction, following the slash and spread or overlap procedure described previously. Tape all changes securely.

Checkpoints
Now you are almost ready for the tissue fit—just a few steps remain.
• Double-check the side seam length on both the bodice front and back, to make sure they are the same. Close the bust dart and fold under seam allowances on the back, to make measuring more accurate. Line up the armhole points and make sure the side waist points match. Blend, if need be, to make both side seams the same length at the waist.
• Check and correct all seam allowances, adding tissue if necessary. There should be 5/8-inch (16-mm) seam allowances at the neckline and armhole seams, and

1-inch (2.5-cm) seam allowances at the shoulders, side seams, and waistline.

- Check that all tape is secure.
- Record all changes on the Personal Measurement Chart.

THE TISSUE FIT

The tissue fit is a step that most homesewers typically skip, but it can save you from time-consuming and expensive mistakes. If extra

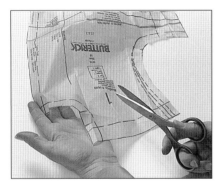

To prepare pattern for the tissue fit, the seam allowances are clipped along curves.

fabric must be added after a garment is cut out, your only option is to re-cut the piece. With the wonders of removable tape and extra tissue, however, you can add and subtract to your tissue pattern until perfection is achieved.

To prepare the pattern for this next step, you may need to re-iron. Be sure to work with a barely warm dry iron and pressing cloth on the wrong side (away from the tape), because the tape can melt very easily. Clip the tissue to the seamline around the neckline, armhole, and waistline

curves. Using the method described earlier, fold and pin all darts closed. When pinning seams together on the tissue, bring the seam allowances to the outside to allow for more flexibility in adjusting them.

For the tissue fitting you should again be wearing the garments and undergarments you wore for the measuring phase. Re-tie the elastic around your waist, snugly but not tight enough to distort, and another piece around your bustline. In addition to acting as points of reference, these will help to anchor the half bodice that your fitting pattern has now become. Gently put on the tissue bodice and have your fitting buddy pin it at the front and back

center stitching lines. The Burda and Style patterns do not have front seams in the bodice, so the edge of the pattern should come exactly to your center front. Now you and your fitting buddy must study the fit of the bodice. Remembering that every action has a reaction, you should evaluate and make any adjustments at the top of the pattern and work your way down.

Checkpoints

- Are there any wrinkles or gaps?
- Does any section seem unduly tight or loose?
- Observe whether the shoulder seam needs to be lengthened or shortened or moved forward.

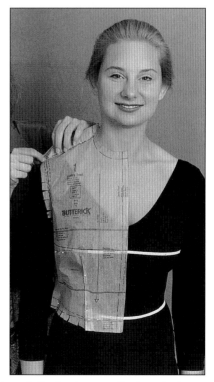

Tissue fit in progress. Amanda does not need the bust cup adjustment at left; it was corrected for a better fit, as shown at right.

- Evaluate the front chest and upper back: are there extra folds of tissue or signs of stress in either area? These would indicate the need for an alteration.
- Check the fit of the neckline. Does it feel comfortable and follow the natural curve of the body? Is there any gapping?

ADJUSTMENTS TO FRONT AND BACK SHOULDER

Up to this point, the shoulder has not been altered. After observing this area, if you determine that a correction is needed, there are two methods to consider—the wedge slash and pivot method or the L-slash method. Refer to Chapter One for detailed instructions for both methods.

First, observe whether the shoulder seam needs to be lengthened or shortened, and then evaluate the front chest and across the back for extra folds of tissue or signs of stress—these would indicate the need for an alteration. If the length of the shoulder seam is within $^1/_2$ inch (1.25 cm) of the length on you between the neck and shoulder points, use the wedge slash and pivot method to make the adjustment. If both the shoulder seam and chest need correction, use the L-slash method to make the adjustment.

It is possible that the shoulder area needs a wedge slash correction in the front and an L-slash correction in the back, or the other way

around. Keep in mind, however, that the same amount of correction must be made to both the front and back shoulder seam, so that the two seams will be the same length when sewn together. Also, keep in mind that the prominent upper back curve alteration may have widened the shoulder dart or created a dart if none had existed. If this is the case, the back shoulder seam will need to be eased or darted into the front shoulder seam. The back alteration at the shoulder seam, however, must still equal any correction made to the front.

ADJUSTMENTS FOR SLOPING OR SQUARE SHOULDERS

Perhaps you and your fitting buddy noted that you have sloping shoulders. If you generally add shoulder pads to your garments to correct for this problem, you may not need to make an adjustment to the pattern. If you have sloping or

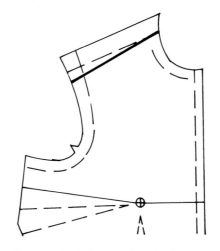

Figure 13. Adjusting for sloping shoulders.

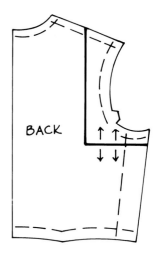

Figure 14. L-slash alteration for sloping or square shoulders.

square shoulders, you can redraw the shoulder seams up to $^1/_4$ inch (6 mm) lower or higher at both the front and back shoulder points. See Figure 13. This small amount will not have a significant effect on the length of the armhole. If, however, the armhole seam will be changed by more than $^1/_4$ inch (6 mm), use the L-slash method to make the adjustment.

The L-slash method for this alteration, however, has one difference: the lower slash line extends into the side seam below the armhole on the front and back. See Figure 14. Move the L-section down for sloping shoulders or up for square shoulders.

ADJUSTMENTS FOR FORWARD SHOULDERS

You may want to put the tissue back on to check whether you need this alteration. Look at your fitting buddy from the side to see if her shoulders tilt forward, and have her check you for the same feature. The neck point should be in line with the ear lobe; the shoulder point at the end of the shoulder seam should be positioned at the center of the upper arm.

There are two common shoulder seam alteration options. The first is, if the entire seam falls further back, it must be redrawn in a more forward position. Move the seam down in front until it falls in the proper place; add the same amount in the back. This will move the entire back seam up. Use the second option if the neck point is in the proper position, but the shoulder point must be moved forward. Re-pin the seam until you have achieved the proper alignment. Then redraw the seamline, making it a straight line between the original neck point and the new shoulder point on both front and back. In either case, if the shoulder point has been moved forward, you will also have to move the circle at the top of the sleeve cap forward an equivalent amount.

ADJUSTMENTS FOR BODICE BACK DARTS

Deepening the back waist darts at their base will compensate for the greater curve of a swayback or slightly rounded upper back. Remember, however, that any waist circumference you eliminate here must be added at the side seam. Deepening the base of the shoulder

dart might also help accommodate a moderately rounded back, but you must compensate for any reduction in the shoulder seamline by lengthening it at the shoulder point until it matches the front when the dart is pinned closed, and then redrawing the armhole as needed. Every time you change the width of a dart, you must adjust and redraw it, and compare it to its matching seam to be certain that both are still the same length.

ADJUSTMENTS FOR NECKLINE

You might need to lower the neckline in front if you habitually hold your head in a forward position or have unusually broad or straight shoulders. This can be accomplished by deepening the

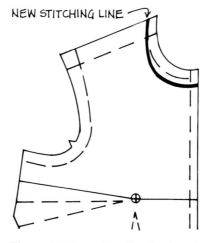

NEW STITCHING LINE

Figure 15. Lowering the front neckline.

neckline clips in the tissue until they reach the collar bones and then redrawing a lower stitching line. See Figure 15.

Checkpoints

• Check any bust cup, bust point, bust dart, or length changes you have made. The telltale signs of a problem are unwanted wrinkles, folds, or stress points. If you notice gapping along the armhole and tightness across the fullest part of the bust, you may need to make the bust cup correction, if you have not already done so, or more or less correction than you have already made.

• Evaluate all darts, seams, and areas you have already altered (you will be forever grateful for removable tape!). You may need to lengthen, shorten, or move darts. Using yet another color, re-mark any stitching lines and record all changes to the nearest $1/8$ inch (3 mm) on both the pattern tissue and Personal Measurement Chart.

• Look at the side seams and waistline curve. You may discover that some of the correction you made in waist circumference at the side seams should be transferred to the waist darts, a common problem if you have a full front waistline. You may notice stress lines coming from the waist darts near the waist. If so, narrow the waist dart by $1/4$ inch (6 mm) up to $1/2$ inch (1.25 cm) on either side of the dart and redraw the dart legs.

• Check to be sure that the waist darts point toward, but do not reach, the bust point.

• Study the waistline curve. If the stitching line for the waistline does not correspond to the actual curve on your body, redraw this line as a dashed stitching line. If your waist is shorter than the pattern's in one area, you may need to slightly extend the clips and adjust the waistline seam. If it is longer, note this and you can tape some of the clips down to reflect the correct line.

• Check the back darts, bust and waist circumference, waistline curve, and length. Check the back curve, especially if you have not made the upper back alteration; you may notice gapping at the neckline and/or along the armhole seam. Check also to see if the center back is pulling up. All of these are indicators that you need to do the major back correction described above. If you already did the correction, make any needed adjustments to eliminate gapping or hiking up. Record all changes on the tissue and the Personal Measurement Chart.

Take off the tissue. Complete any changes you found necessary, redraw all stitching and cutting lines, and adjust seam allowances if necessary. Re-pin and re-fit, continuing to fine tune and record all changes until you are satisfied. Now, at last, you are ready to lay out and cut the muslin.

THE MUSLIN

Before laying out the pattern pieces on the muslin, remove all pins from the seams and darts, and return the tissue to its original flat condition. This may need to be followed with a light touch of a barely warm iron and pressing cloth on the wrong side. It is especially important to iron out any little flaps resulting from the slashing around the curved seams.

If your pre-washed muslin fabric has been in storage for a while, it may need ironing. Check to be certain that the lengthwise center fold is exactly in the center, that selvages meet exactly, and that the grain is true. You may have noted that fitting patterns sometimes suggest using gingham fabric instead of muslin. We find the gingham checks more of a distraction than a help and have noticed that, because they are printed

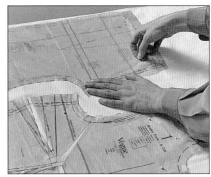

The altered pattern pieces are carefully pinned to the muslin. To make this bodice pattern close in the back rather than the front, a seam allowance is added to the center back. The center front seamline is then placed on the fold, eliminating the seam allowance.

on the cloth rather than woven into it, the lines do not necessarily follow the grain of the fabric.

Once the fabric and tissue have been properly prepared, lay out and

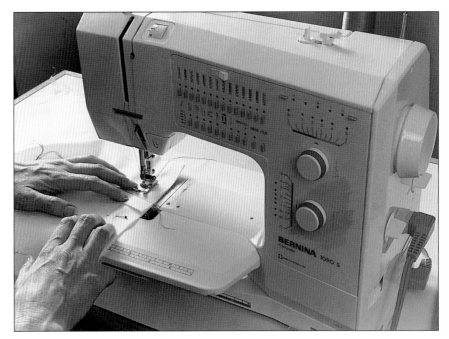

When sewing the muslin, the machine is set to a long stitch length so stitching can be easily removed if further alterations are needed.

cut the bodice according to the manufacturer's directions, taking care to allow the seam allowances we have suggested. Use a tracing wheel and colored transfer paper to transfer all notches, bust point, darts, and seamlines to the wrong side of the fabric. These markings will help with accuracy.

The next step is very important. **Set your sewing machine to a long stitching length—3 or 4 mm on European machines or the fewest number of stitches per inch on other machines.** The automatic stitch lengths on many fine machines are designed for sewing secure seams, but this very security makes them difficult to remove if an adjustment must be made.

When you sew the muslin together for the first time, do not back stitch at the beginning or ends of seamlines—instead, leave the thread tails. Be very careful to follow the stitching lines exactly or you will have wasted all that time spent to ensure precise measurements. Reinforce the neckline by stitching along the seamline. The Vogue and Butterick fitting patterns are designed to have a center front opening, but we suggest that you stitch this seam closed and leave the center back seam open. Because the more difficult fitting problems tend to occur in the front, a closed center front will be a better test of fitting quality.

Once the muslin bodice has been assembled, clip to the seamline along the neck, armhole, and waist curves, press open seams and darts toward the center or down. Try the

During the muslin fit, all alterations are evaluated and further adjustments are made until the bodice fits perfectly.

bodice on right side out. Have your fitting buddy pin the back closure along the seamline and, together, take a critical look at what you have achieved. If you have done the preliminary steps with care and attention to detail, you should have only minor adjustments to make at this point. Pin-fit any changes to seams and darts, and redraw neck and waistline seams if necessary.

When you take off the muslin, be sure to mark any such changes on the wrong side and transfer these changes to the pattern tissue. Make any needed adjustments and re-fit to be sure the bodice is now free of wrinkles, gaps, and stress points. You have now passed the halfway point toward that once-elusive goal—your clothes fitting like couture garments. Congratulations!

Chapter Six

Fitting the sleeve

"I knew the sleeves weren't right, and I tried to fix them. Now I can't move!"

—*Nancy, a G Street Fabrics staff member*

If you have ever reached forward and heard the telltale "snap" of breaking threads, you know how important well-fitting sleeves can be. Every pattern includes extra ease around the sleeve cap for freedom of movement, but you might require more than the pattern's. You may have longer-than-average or shorter-than-average arms; you will need to lengthen or shorten most sleeves. Or, you may have well-developed upper arms; you will need to add circumference so that the sleeves are not too tight. Whatever the adjustment, appropriate sleeve alterations will result in greater comfort, freedom of movement, and better appearance.

MINOR ADJUSTMENTS TO SLEEVE

Common fitting problems in long set-in sleeves are length and width, especially of the upper arm. Of these corrections, lengthening or shortening and making exterior corrections to the underarm seam are minor and relatively easy. Providing additional bicep room is more complex; two methods for making this alteration will be described.

All of the commercial fitting patterns have two sets of parallel lengthen/shorten lines on the sleeves, and all except the Style, Simplicity, and McCall's patterns also provide an elbow dart (Simplicity and McCall's patterns indicate the point

---

Basic Fitting Terms

Review the following terms from Chapter One: ALTERATION LINE, CROSSWISE GRAIN, FASHION RULER™, GRAINLINE, GUIDELINE, HORIZONTAL, LENGTHWISE GRAIN, and VERTICAL. Review from Chapter Two: ARMHOLE POINT, CAP LINE, CAP OF SLEEVE, EASE ALLOWANCE, and FITTING EASE.

CAP HEIGHT. The distance between the bicep or cap line and the shoulder point.

at which the elbow should be). Make needed length alterations at these lines rather than at the bottom of the sleeve. Referring to the Personal Measurement Chart in Chapter Three, compare your shoulder-to-elbow (#10) and elbow-to-wrist (#11) measurements to those of the pattern. If you are using Style, add your two body measurements and compare to the total measurement on the pattern. Make any needed length adjustments. It is not uncommon to have to lengthen or shorten above the elbow, but do the opposite below the elbow, to position the elbow dart correctly. These are all considered minor adjustments.

A minor bicep circumference alteration can be made to the underarm seam, but only if an alteration was made to the bodice side seams. The distance between the armhole point and the notches must match on both the sleeve and the bodice. If you made an adjustment to the bodice side seams at the armhole point, you must now add or subtract the same amount to the underarm seams of the sleeve at the armhole point. See Figure 1. Unless you will need to do the major bicep alteration, blend and true the seamlines from the new armhole point to the original wrist line. If there is an elbow dart, it should be folded closed. When redrawing the underarm seam, remember to add 1-inch (2.5-cm)

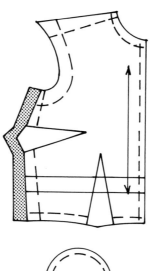

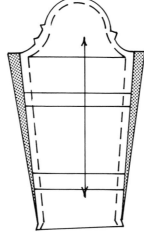

Figure 1. Adding circumference to underarm, to equal bodice circumference addition.

seam allowances.

Vogue, Butterick, McCall's, and Burda patterns all have very similar sleeves. The Style and Simplicity patterns, in addition to having no elbow dart, have a flatter sleeve cap. Style does not have any ease at the elbow, to allow for a bending arm, but it is fuller through the bicep. In comparing the Style bodice with the others, we notice it also has a markedly lower armhole point. The

flatter cap and greater width, therefore, compensate for the lack of ease or an elbow dart.

Compare your bicep circumference (#5 on the Personal Measurement Chart) with that of the pattern. If your bicep measurement plus the required ease approximates that of your pattern once you have made any underarm corrections, no further adjustment is needed at this point.

If you have already determined that you do not require any further width adjustment and have made the needed length adjustment, proceed to the tissue fit.

MAJOR ADJUSTMENTS TO SLEEVE

If your biceps need more room or are thin, the sleeve will either pull and strain, especially when the arms are in a forward position, or it will hang limply and look empty. Correcting these problems is a bit more complicated and is considered a major adjustment.

BICEP CIRCUMFERENCE ADJUSTMENT

Compared with major adjustments to the bodice, these are a walk in the park! There are two methods that will correct problems of bicep circumference. Both are major adjustments because they cause more than one area to change—the shape of the armhole seam and the width of the sleeve at the bicep.

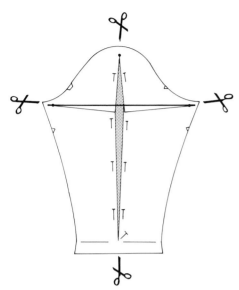

Figure 2. Adding circumference to bicep.

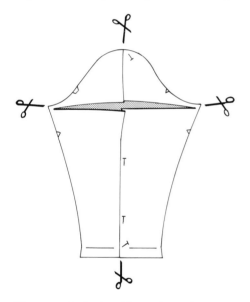

Figure 3. Reducing bicep circumference.

Adding Width: Method One

If you need to change 1 inch (2.5 cm) or less in the sleeve width at the bicep or cap line, make this interior alteration, following these steps:

1. Draw a line down the center of the sleeve from the shoulder point to the hemline, parallel to the grainline.

2. Clip the seam allowances opposite the ends of the line you just drew, to create hinges at the shoulder point and hem.

3. Clip the seam allowances to, but not through, the armhole point on either side.

4. Beginning at the center, slash along the bicep line to, but not through, the armhole point on either side.

5. Beginning at the center, slash down the line you drew to the hemline and up to the shoulder point, leaving hinges at both ends.

6. The pattern is now very fragile, held together by four tiny hinges—at the shoulder point, hemline, and armhole points. Carefully place the pattern over tissue on the cork or foam core mat, putting a pin through the hemline hinge.

7. To add width up to 1 inch (2.5 cm) at the bicep or cap line, pull the pattern apart to create an opening along the center slash. The edges of the bicep slash will overlap and the sleeve cap will shorten. See Figure 2. Pin and tape the pattern pieces in place.

8. To reduce width, gently overlap the edges of the center slash up to 1 inch (2.5 cm). In this case, the bicep slash will open up and the sleeve cap will become taller. See Figure 3. Pin and tape the pattern pieces in place.

After performing this adjustment, the sleeve cap height will be altered; therefore, the original height must be restored. To do so, follow these steps:

1. Measure the total armhole seam lengths of the sleeve and the front and back bodice. Compare these measurements; there should be approximately 1 inch (2.5 cm) additional ease in the sleeve cap. Restoring the sleeve cap height will also add to or subtract from the cap ease. Take care when adding here, because the bicep adjustment below also adds to the sleeve cap ease.

2. If you need more or less length around the sleeve cap, draw a horizontal line through the sleeve cap about halfway between the notches on either side and the shoulder point; slash along this line.

3. If you have added fullness to the sleeve at the bicep, place the pattern over extra tissue on the cork or foam core mat and spread the two parts the amount the bicep line overlapped or to add up to 2 inches (5 cm) of ease. If you have decreased fullness, overlap the two parts the same distance that the edges of the cap line slash spread apart or the amount of necessary additional ease up to 1 inch (2.5 cm). See Figure 4.

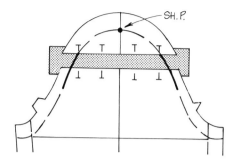

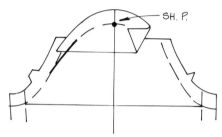

Figure 4. Restoring original sleeve cap height. At top, sleeve cap is raised after circumference is added to bicep; at bottom, sleeve cap is lowered after reducing bicep circumference.

4. Pin and tape in place; blend and true the sleeve cap stitching line.

Adding Width: Method Two

If, after you have completed the above method, you still need more width, you will also need to follow this method, which is used when more than 1 inch (2.5 cm) must be added. This method is a variation of the L-slash; follow these steps:

1. Draw two parallel lines on either side of the center line of the sleeve and about 2 inches (5 cm) apart. These lines should extend from the cutting line of the sleeve cap to 1 inch (2.5 cm) below the bicep or cap line.

2. From the bottom of each line, square a line and extend it to the underarm seamline, forming an "L" on each side of the sleeve; slash along each "L." See Figure 5. NOTE: Do not use the bicep line for this purpose.

3. Place the pattern pieces over tissue and pin the center section to the cork or foam core mat.

4. To add width, spread each L-section away from the center one-half of the total needed distance, keeping the slashed edges parallel to the center line. See Figure 6.

5. Pin and tape all sections in place; blend and true all seamlines and cutting lines as necessary.

6. Re-measure the bicep line to be sure you have added the correct amount.

Checkpoints

If you have made either of the above alterations to the sleeve cap and/or you have changed anything about the shape of the armhole on the bodice, you must double-check that all important points still match. Major alterations to sleeve width at the bicep or cap line can add extra ease to the sleeve cap. Alterations to the shape of the armhole can change the way the sleeve fits into it. Before proceeding to the tissue fit, reevaluate these areas to see how they relate to one another:

• Check the shoulder seams of the bodice, both front and back. Have they been moved forward? If so, the

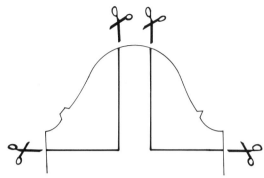

Figure 5. L-slash cutting lines for bicep circumference alteration.

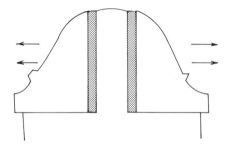

Figure 6. L-slash sections are moved out to add circumference at bicep.

circle at the shoulder point on the sleeve pattern must be moved forward an equivalent amount.

• Re-measure and compare the armhole seamlines of both the front bodice and front sleeve. The armhole seam of the sleeve should be $1/2$ to 1 inch (1.25 to 2.5 cm) bigger than that of the bodice; easing the sleeve into the armhole will be difficult if the difference is greater. On the other hand, movement will be restricted if the difference is less. Check the back armhole and the back of the sleeve cap with the same ease consideration in mind.

• Check the distribution of the ease. If there is an unequal distribution, move the shoulder point forward or backward to even it out.

- If the sleeve does not meet the minimum requirements for ease, add to the sleeve cap height and/or slash and spread open. If the sleeve cap is much bigger, you can extend the ease toward the notches. Keep in mind that most fabrics will ease better than muslin.
- Provide a seam allowance of 1 inch (2.5 cm) under the arm and $^5/_8$ inch (16 mm) at the sleeve cap.

THE TISSUE FIT

Before trying on the sleeve, touch it up on the wrong side with a barely warm iron and pressing cloth if the tissue has wrinkled. If your pattern has an elbow dart, fold and pin it as you did the darts on the bodice. Pin the sleeve seam allowance to the outside and try the

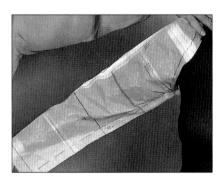

Tissue fit in progress.

sleeve on your right arm. You might want to put the bodice on, to help position the top of the sleeve.

Checkpoints

- Study the fullness of the sleeve cap, ease around the bicep, place-

ment of the elbow dart (if any), and whether the hemline hits exactly at the wrist.

- Check the hang of the sleeve. If you notice vertical folds that point toward the cap, add up to an additional $^1/_2$ inch (1.25 cm) to the sleeve cap height.

Make any other changes, mark them on the tissue and note them on the Personal Measurement Chart. Double-check your corrections by trying the sleeve on once more.

THE MUSLIN

Following the same procedure you used for the bodice, lay out and cut the sleeves, transfer all markings and seamlines, and baste the darts and

The muslin sleeve is tried on by itself, to evaluate all sleeve adjustments.

seams. Try the right sleeve on once more, turning seam allowances to the inside and slightly easing the sleeve cap. Make sure that the ease in the sleeve cap is adequate and the sleeve hangs well.

Make and record any changes. Follow the pattern's directions to set the sleeves into the bodice, taking care to evenly distribute ease between the notches and the shoulder point, and to sew exactly on the seamlines. Try on the bodice, now complete with sleeves, one more time. Check for any stitching accidents as well as fitting problems, since both will be easier to correct now—before you attach the skirt.

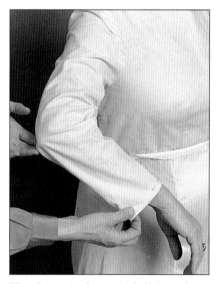

The sleeve is then stitched into the muslin bodice, to evaluate the fit of the entire bodice.

Chapter Seven

Fitting the skirt

"Me?! A flat bottom? Since when?"...After a glance in the mirror: "Oops! What *was* in back is now in front!"

—*Mary, a G Street Fabrics staff member*

If you page quickly through this chapter, you will see that many of the alteration procedures have already been explained in earlier chapters. Happily, there are also fewer skirt corrections than bodice, sleeve, or pants corrections. Although there are some major, as well as minor, skirt adjustments sometimes required, they are needed less often. Proceed with confidence—you are almost done!

Before beginning to make specific adjustments, compare your waist and hip measurements. These two areas are closely related to one another, like the waist and bust areas of the bodice. The amount of correction needed in one area as compared to the other will help you determine which alterations to make.

ADJUSTMENTS TO SKIRT WAIST CIRCUMFERENCE

There are three methods to achieve the proper circumference at the waist: minor exterior adjustment, minor dart adjustment, and major interior correction.

METHOD ONE: EXTERIOR ADJUSTMENT

This method of adjusting waist circumference is considered a minor alteration. As with the side seams of the bodice, you can add up to 1 inch (2.5 cm) at the side seam to each pattern piece, for a total of 4 inches (10 cm). Review the exception to this general rule as explained in Chapter Five on page 56. Begin by adding to or subtracting from each side seam at the waist exactly what you added to or sub-

Basic Fitting Terms

Review the following terms from Chapter One: ALTERATION LINE, CROSSWISE GRAIN, DART, FASHION RULER™, FLEXIBLE RULER, GUIDELINE, HIP CURVE, HORIZONTAL, LENGTHWISE GRAIN, and VERTICAL. Review from Chapter Two: CENTER LINE, HIGH HIPLINE, HIP DEPTH, LOW HIPLINE, and SIDE WAIST POINT.

tracted from the side seam of the bodice at the waist point. See Figure 1. NOTE: Before choosing this method, consider Method Three. If you need more than 1 inch (2.5 cm) and cannot coordinate this correction with needed hip alterations for Method Three, proceed to Method Two.

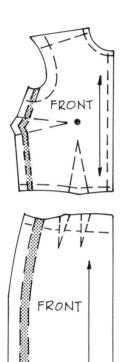

Figure 1. Adding width at side seams of bodice and skirt.

METHOD TWO: ADJUSTMENT OF DARTS

This method of adjusting waist circumference is considered a minor alteration. You can add or subtract to the skirt waist dart(s) the equiva-

lent of any additions or subtractions that were made to the bodice waist darts. You may take a dart out entirely or make a too-wide dart that pokes out into two smaller darts. Consider using this method in combination with Method One or Three.

Remember that to retain the darts' original relationship to one another and to the center lines, the distance at the waistline from the center to the closest dart leg should be the same in both the bodice and the skirt. If the distance is not the same, the skirt dart must be moved. If there are two front skirt darts, the inside leg of the inside dart should line up with the inside leg of the bodice waist dart. See Figure 2.

If the skirt dart or darts must be moved, follow these steps:

1. Draw a box around both darts. The vertical sides of the box are parallel to the center line, and the horizontal bottom of the box is drawn just under the longest dart. See Figure 3.

2. Slash along all three sides of the box.

3. Over tissue on the cork or foam core mat, slide the box to the right or left until the dart nearest the center front matches up with the bodice waist dart.

4. Pin and tape in place.

5. Pin or tape the skirt front darts closed and blend the waistline seam as needed.

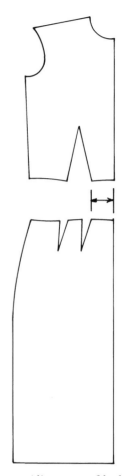

Figure 2. Alignment of bodice and skirt waist darts.

Figure 3. Moving skirt darts.

METHOD THREE: INTERIOR CORRECTION

If you need to add or subtract more circumference to the waist than can be achieved by either of the two methods described above, you can use an interior correction. This method of adjusting waist circumference is considered a major alteration, because it will also affect the hip circumference. However, if you need more or less width at the waist, it is likely that you also need more or less width at the hip.

This correction is especially effective for a very slim individual who needs to subtract circumference. It can also be used to adjust for a flat seat or to compensate for full hips or thighs. Note particularly how much change you need to make in each area after having made the exterior changes and dart adjustments described above, or consider this alteration instead of or in conjunction with the other methods.

Referring to the Personal Measurement Chart in Chapter Three, locate the alteration measurement for the following areas: high front hip (#4A) and low back hip (#4B).

The interior alteration will be "even"–opened up or overlapped equally. For example, if you need to make a total change of 2 inches (5 cm) at the front waist and $2^1/2$ inches (6.5 cm) at the high front hip, you can make an even interior change of 2 inches (5 cm) to alter the waist and most of the hip; then add the remaining $1/2$ inch (1.25 cm) needed at the hip with an exterior change. If you have a prominent tummy or seat curve, you could alternatively make an interior correction for the entire $2^1/2$ inches (6.5 cm) and then enlarge the waist darts to absorb the additional $1/2$ inch (1.25 cm).

If, in the back, you need to subtract 1 inch (2.5 cm) at the waist and 2 inches (5 cm) at the low hip, you can make an even interior adjustment that subtracts 1 inch (2.5 cm) from both areas and then subtract the remaining 1 inch (2.5 cm) from the hip with an exterior change. If you have a flat seat, you could alternatively make the larger 2-inch (5-cm) adjustment to the hip and make the waist darts smaller.

You will find that this adjustment is very similar to lengthening or shortening, except that it is performed vertically rather than horizontally. Once you have determined the necessary amount of change, follow these steps:

1. Draw a line from waist to hem, about $1^1/2$ inches (4 cm) in from the side seam and parallel to the grainline. Be careful to avoid the darts.

2. Draw a guideline at a right angle to the slash line, or use the lengthen/shorten line for this purpose.

3. Slash along the entire length of this line, dividing the front or back skirt pattern into two sections. See Figure 4.

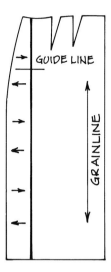

Figure 4. Interior alteration to adjust circumference.

4. If you are adding width, place the two pattern sections over tissue on the cork or foam core mat. Pin and tape one section to the tissue, draw the alteration line, and extend the guideline. If you are subtracting width, you will not need the tissue, but you will need to draw an alteration line.

5. To add width, spread the edges apart, keeping the cut edges parallel to each other and matching alteration line and guideline.

6. To subtract width, overlap the cut edges the needed amount, keeping the cut edges parallel to each other and matching alteration line and guideline.

7. Pin and tape in place; blend the waist seamline and hemline.

ADJUSTMENTS TO SKIRT HIP CIRCUMFERENCE

There are two methods to achieve the proper circumference at the hip: minor exterior adjustment and major interior correction.

METHOD ONE: EXTERIOR ADJUSTMENT

This method of adjusting hip circumference is considered a minor alteration and is dependent on the exterior width adjustment at the waist. You can change the hip circumference by adding or subtracting up to 1 inch (2.5 cm) at the side seamline. If you have made a 1-inch (2.5-cm) exterior adjustment at the waist, you can make the same amount of correction at the hip plus up to an additional 1 inch (2.5 cm). See Figure 5.

To review the general rule of 1 inch (2.5 cm), for example, if you have added $^1/_2$ inch (1.25 cm) at the waist, you can add up to 1$^1/_2$ inches (4 cm) at the hip. On the other hand, if you have subtracted 1 inch (2.5 cm) at the waist, you can subtract up to 2 inches (5 cm) at the hip.

What makes the skirt an interesting challenge is that the side seam, unlike that in the bodice, has its own distinctive curve, just as you do. Remember when you were studying your figure in the full-length mirror? You may have noticed relatively little hip curve; your figure descends along the sides

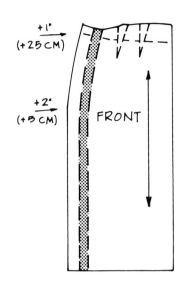

Figure 5. Exterior alteration to add circumference.

in almost straight lines. Or, you may have discovered that what curve you do have is relatively low, in the vicinity of your fullest point in back. Your hip curve may be relatively high, coming almost straight out from the waist. This common and delightful variety is why the hip curve ruler was invented; its side has a varying degree of curve so that you can select the section that most closely resembles you. For a high hip curve, use the curvy end of the ruler; for a low hip curve with full thighs, use the more gently curved end of the ruler. Begin drawing the new side seam from the waist, moving down past the fullest part of the hip, and then straight down to the hem, to preserve the line of the skirt.

METHOD TWO: INTERIOR CORRECTION

This alteration, described in detail above in the section about altering waist circumference, is considered major because it affects circumference at both the waist and hip. Because it is an even alteration that extends the entire length of the skirt, it is effective if you must add or subtract more than 1 inch (2.5 cm) at both the waist and hip. If you need to make this correction, review the steps on page 71. Once you have made the interior correction, you may need to blend the waist seam with the Fashion Ruler or hip curve.

ADJUSTMENTS TO SKIRT LENGTH

In keeping with the general plan of attack to work from the top down, length will be the last consideration before proceeding to the tissue fit. Because the skirt is straight, you may add or subtract length at the bottom edge. The steps to follow are easy:

1. Referring to the Personal Measurement chart, compare your waist-to-knee measurement (#9) to that of the pattern, measuring along the side seamline.

2. To lengthen, add tissue and draw an alteration line the needed distance below the hemline and parallel to it; extend the center line, seamlines, and cutting lines down to meet it.

3. To shorten, draw an alteration line the needed distance above the hemline and parallel to it, intersecting the center line, seamlines, and cutting lines. Cut away the excess hem length or fold the hemline, bring it up to meet the line you just drew, and tape in place.

4. For the tissue and muslin fittings, you may cut off the hem allowance. If you wish to keep it, the standard hem allowance for a straight skirt is 2 to 3 inches (5 to 7.5 cm).

THE TISSUE FIT

Following the same procedures you used for the bodice and sleeves, prepare the pattern for the tissue fit. Add 1-inch (2.5-cm) seam allowances to waist and side seams, and $^5/_8$-inch (16-mm) seam allowances to center seams.

Checkpoints

• Check to see if the front and back side seams line up with one another. If they do not, make any needed adjustment at the waistline rather than the hemline.

• Tie a strip of elastic around your waist. This will act like a waistband and help define your actual waistline. Check carefully that the side seam is properly situated on your body. If necessary, reattach the plumb lines under your arms to double-check this alignment.

• Check also to see that the hem falls evenly. If you have made the

Tissue fit in progress.

corrections accurately, it should.

If the hem does not fall evenly, have your fitting buddy pull down on the front hem until it is even. This will bring the waist down past your natural waistline. If the gap created is $^1/_2$ inch (1.25 cm) or more, you will need to make the major abdomen curve adjustment on page 75. If the gap is less than $^1/_2$ inch (1.25 cm), redraw the front waistline as described below.

If the problem with the hemline is in back, your fitting buddy should pull down on the back hem until it is even. Again, to add $^1/_2$ inch (1.25 cm) or more, make the major seat curve adjustment on page 76. If it is less than $^1/_2$ inch (1.25 cm), redraw the back waistline as described

below. To make the hem horizontal and sides vertical, some individuals may have to pull the back waist up above the natural waistline. This fitting problem indicates a swayback; the waist seamline and cutting lines will have to be redrawn to accurately reflect this figure variation. Keep in mind that while pulling the hemline up or down, try to keep it exactly horizontal to the ground and the side seamlines perpendicular to the ground. The waistline seam, however, may not remain horizontal; instead, it will follow the natural line of your body.

REDRAWING FRONT OR BACK WAISTLINE CURVES

To raise the waistline, follow these steps:

1. Unpin the skirt darts.

2. Tape any prior clipping closed and add a strip of extra tissue, if necessary.

3. At the center front, measure up to the natural waistline and make a mark on the extra tissue.

4. Put the tissue on and adjust the hemline so it is horizontal to the ground, lowering the waist below your natural waistline.

5. Take the tissue off; fold the darts closed, and pin or tape them temporarily.

6. Use the curved ruler to connect the side waist point, which has remained unchanged, with the new mark at center front. Make the curve as gentle as possible. See Figure 6.

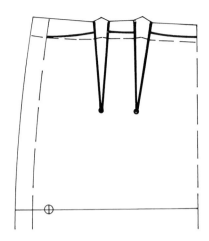

Figure 6. Raising the waistline.

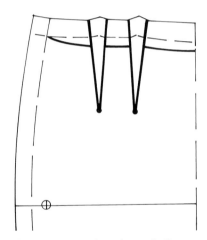

Figure 7. Lowering the waistline.

7. Correct seam allowance to 1 inch (2.5 cm) and trim away any excess tissue before re-opening the darts.

Lowering the waistline is more commonly done in the back, to correct for a swayback. To lower the waistline, follow these steps:

1. Adjust the hemline so it is horizontal to the ground. At the center back, measure down to the natural waistline and re-mark the waistline.

2. Take tissue off, keeping the darts closed.

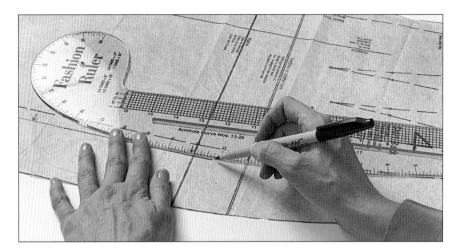

The French curve is used to neaten the hip curve stitching line after alterations have been made and evaluated during the tissue fit. The two different ends of the French curve can be used, depending on whether the hip curve is low (top) or curve is high (bottom).

3. Use the curved ruler to connect the side waist point, which has remained unchanged, and blend the waistline with the new mark at center back. Be sure not to make the new waistline too scooped; the back waist is usually a very subtle curve. See Figure 7.

4. Correct the seam allowance to 1 inch (2.5 cm) and trim away any excess tissue before re-opening the darts.

Checkpoints

• Evaluate the curve over your hips at the side seams. Does the hip curve of the tissue match the hip curve of your body? If need be, redraw the stitching line to reflect your hip curve more accurately. When you take the tissue off, use the French curve or Fashion Ruler to neaten this line.

• Reverse the tissue and try it on the other side to make sure the waistline seam is in the same spot on both sides of your body. Many people have one hip that is slightly higher than the other. If this is the case for you, use two different colors to indicate the right and left seamlines. Use the elastic as a guide to help you achieve the proper curve when marking a new waistline.

When you are satisfied that you have made all the necessary adjustments, take off the tissue, neaten and record any changes, and double-check the fit one last time. If you do not need to make a major adjustment for a prominent front or back curve, you are ready to lay out and cut the skirt muslin, following the same procedures you used before, and to transfer all pattern markings and seamlines. If you do need to make a prominent curve adjustment, continue with the major correction described below.

MAJOR CORRECTION FOR ABDOMEN CURVES

The most common major adjustment, especially for older women, is the alteration for a prominent raised abdomen. As mentioned earlier, no amount of exercise or dieting can prevent this perfectly natural shift in the figure's shape. Clothes that have been properly adjusted, however, actually make the abdomen appear less prominent because the alteration adds length and width where needed.

Have you stopped wearing skirts and pants with side pockets because you do not like the way they gap? Do your skirts and pants tend to ride up at the center front, or do they pull down below your abdomen, making skirt hems uneven and the crotch of pants uncomfortable? These are sure signs that you need to make an abdominal pattern correction.

This alteration is similar to the bust cup correction described in Chapter Five. It provides both additional length and width to cover a larger curve than the pattern-maker anticipated. To successfully make the adjustment for this very common figure characteristic, follow these steps:

1. Draw a horizontal line from the center front to the point of the nearest dart.

2. If there is a second dart, continue the line to the point of this dart. If the second dart is longer or shorter than the first, angle this section of the line slightly to arrive at the dart point.

3. Continue the line diagonally up to the side waist point.

4. Extend the mid-line of each dart to, but not through, each dart point.

5. From the center front, slash along the horizontal line and then along the diagonal line up to, but not through, the side waist point.

6. Clip the seam allowance to create a hinge at the side waist point.

7. Slash along the lines through the center of each dart to, but not through, the dart point, creating a hinge at each dart point.

8. Place the pattern over tissue on the cork or foam core mat, pinning along the lower edge of the horizontal slash and at the waist point hinge.

9. Gently spread the pattern piece up at the waistline to raise the center front up to 1 inch (2.5 cm), to accommodate the abdomen curve. You will notice that the darts open up and a V-shaped opening appears along the diagonal slash to the waist point. See Figure 8.

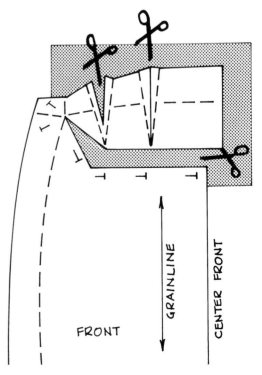

Figure 8. Abdomen curve alteration provides additional length and width to front.

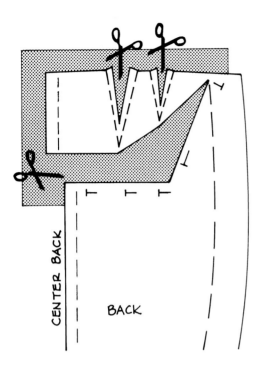

Figure 9. Seat curve alteration provides additional length and width to back.

MAJOR ADJUSTMENT FOR SEAT CURVE

For many individuals, a prominent seat curve is an area of concern. Symptoms of fitting problems in this area include a sensation of tightness in the back, horizontal wrinkles across the back, S-curved side seams, pocket gapping, and hiked-up hemline in the back. The steps described above for the prominent abdomen adjustment can also be performed on the skirt back pattern to correct for a similar problem in back. See Figure 9. After completing the correction, record all changes on the Personal Measurement Chart and the pattern pieces. Once all adjustments for prominent curves have been completed, you're ready to proceed to the muslin fit.

THE MUSLIN

Prepare the pattern as before and lay out the skirt on pre-washed muslin according to the pattern directions. Cut it out, trace all markings, and use the basting stitch to assemble it. Turn seam allowances to the inside. If you have a back opening in the bodice, leave a back opening from the widest point at the low back hipline up to the waistline. Tie a strip of elastic around your waist to act as a waistband.

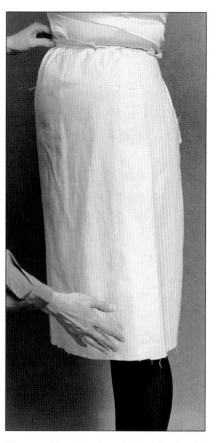

The muslin skirt is tried on by itself, to evaluate all skirt adjustments.

10. Measure to be sure that the two edges of the horizontal slash are exactly parallel and the proper distance apart to make the needed correction.

11. Pin and tape all pieces securely in place.

12. Because this correction moves the center front out, extend the center front all the way to the hemline, adding tissue. This step provides extra width, just as moving the waistline up provided extra length.

13. Record all changes you have made on the Personal Measurement Chart and the pattern pieces.

Try the skirt on and fine tune the fit, marking any needed adjustments both on the muslin and pattern tissue. Pin the skirt to the bodice at the waist seamline, checking to see that all seams and darts match up accurately. Note any needed changes on both the muslin and tissue. Baste in any of these changes and try the skirt on once more.

All that remains now is to baste the skirt and bodice together. Try on the entire dress and have your fitting buddy pin the back closure.

Are you impressed by what really

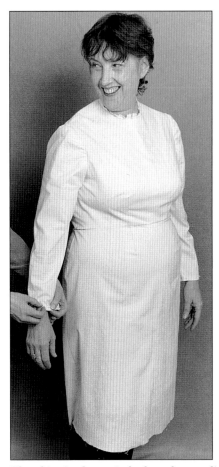 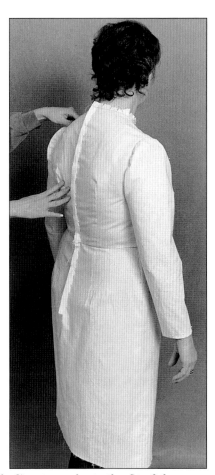

The skirt is then stitched to the muslin bodice, to evaluate the fit of the entire dress.

good fit looks and feels like? Isn't it wonderful? Both you and your fitting buddy should take one last critical look, to be certain that no troublesome wrinkles, gaps, or stress marks remain. If there are some minute adjustments, pin-fit them, mark them on the muslin and tissue, and make them. Save the muslin dress, however, so that you can periodically see if your fitting pattern is still an accurate reflection of the "real you."

In Chapter Nine you will learn how to preserve your fitting pattern and how to use it when you are working with fashion patterns. In Chapter Ten, you will learn more about fitting problems associated with pockets and various types of closures, as well as how to use your fitting pattern to create fashion designs of your own.

Chapter Eight

Fitting pants

"I'd give anything to have a pants pattern that really fits me!"

—Sue, G Street Fabrics
staff member

Before beginning to fashion your own personalized pants fitting pattern, it's a good idea to evaluate the differences in the basic pants patterns provided by the major companies and take a few more personal measurements. The ideal fitting pattern would be for a garment that fits the basic definition of slacks—with 2 to 4 inches (5 to 10 cm) of ease. The jeans fit is too tight to be practical in anything other than the traditional denim or other sturdy cotton fabric. Trousers, culottes, and palazzo pants are so full that they present very few fitting problems, except for extreme variations from the "average" figure. This is probably why they are so popular in ready-to-wear and homesewing patterns. However, there are far more potential fitting problems for the woman who wants the elegance and comfort of classic fitted slacks.

The major companies state that they design for a woman who is five feet six inches (165 cm) tall and, at least in the case of the American companies, has the same standardized bust, waist, and hip measurements. As we found with the basic dress patterns, there are some

intriguing differences. The photographs on page 80 show the front and back pant pattern pieces from Vogue, McCall's, Simplicity, Style, and Burda laid out on a grid.

Note the differences, especially in the crotch curve, crotch depth, shape of the waist curve, and width of the pant leg. Some of these differences can be attributed to the fact that the European patterns (Style and Burda) are designed for a somewhat shorter and rounder body than are the American patterns. Since the Simplicity and Style patterns are not meant to be fitting patterns, design ease also accounts for some of the variations. Indeed, the Simplicity pattern, chosen because it was the only one in the season's catalogue that was a semi-fitted pant with a conventional waistband, allows so much ease as to probably qualify as trousers rather than fitted pants. Differences in what the pattern companies consider to be the minimum amount of wearing ease account for still other variations. Note also the variations in the angle, relative to the grainline, of the center back seam and in the waist, crotch, and hip curves on the pattern pieces.

Basic Fitting Terms

Review the following terms from Chapter One: ALTERATION LINE, DART, FASHION RULER™, GRAINLINE, GUIDELINE, HINGE, HIP CURVE, and SLASH. Review from Chapter Two: CENTER LINE, DESIGN EASE, FITTING EASE, HIGH HIPLINE, HIP DEPTH, LOW HIPLINE, SIDE WAIST POINT, and WAIST DARTS. Review from Chapter Five: DART LEGS and DART WIDTH.

CROTCH DEPTH. The distance along the side seam from the side waist point to the point at which the crotch line intersects the side seamline.

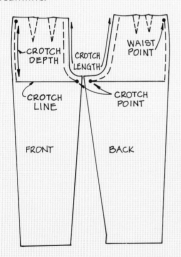

CROTCH EXTENSION. The curved area of the front and back crotch seam that ends at the crotch point and is part of the inseam. The extensions can be longer, as in culottes, or shorter, as in jeans.

CROTCH LENGTH. The distance from the center front waistline down between the legs and back up to the center back waistline. This is also known as stride measurement, as in Burda patterns.

CROTCH LINE. A line drawn parallel to the crosswise grain, from the crotch point to the side seamline on both the front and back of the pants pattern.

CROTCH POINT. The point at which the seamline around the crotch intersects the inside seamline of the pant leg.

CULOTTES. Pants that are so full as to give the illusion of being a flared skirt. Culottes may have soft pleats at the waist and flare into an A-line below the hips.

INSEAM. Measurement taken from the crotch point to just below the inside ankle bone.

JEANS. Pants that are extremely tight-fitting, traditionally allowing little or no ease.

OUTSEAM. Measurement taken from the side waist point to just below the outside ankle bone.

PALAZZO PANTS. Very full pants, usually gathered at the waist and flaring into still more fullness at the hem; usually made of flowing, drapey fabric.

PANTS. Sometimes used interchangeably with "trousers" (see below), this is also the generic word for all garments that, in one way or another, act as divided skirts, encircling each leg separately in fabric.

SLACKS. Pants with waist darts, as opposed to soft pleats, that allow 2 to 4 inches (5 to 10 cm) of ease at the hip. Although looser than jeans, slacks are still relatively tight-fitting.

SOFT PLEAT. Performs much the same function as a dart, but with only the top portion of the dart legs sewn down and the rest left open to allow for additional ease and drape.

TROUSERS. Pants with soft pleats and relatively relaxed fit, with 4 to 6 inches (10 to 15 cm) of ease at the hip.

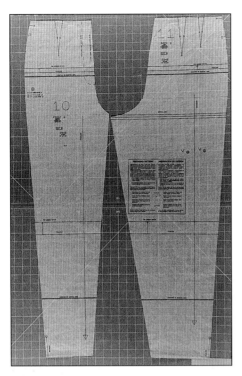

Front and back of Vogue #2946 pants pattern, by permission of The Butterick Co., Inc., New York, NY.

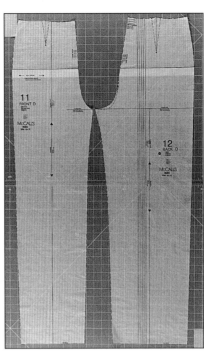

Front and back of McCall's #6985 pants pattern, by permission of Palmer/Pletsch and The McCall Pattern Company, New York, NY.

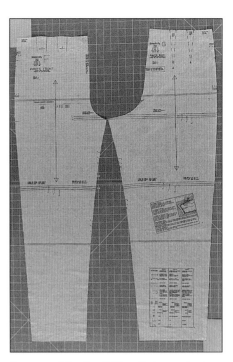

Front and back of Simplicity #8239 pants pattern, by permission of Simplicity Pattern Co., Inc., New York, NY.

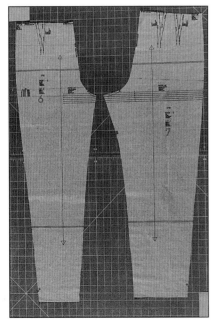

Front and back of Style #2712 pants pattern, by permission of Simplicity Pattern Co., Inc., New York, NY.

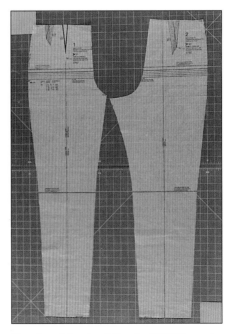

Front and back of Burda #3752 pants pattern, by permission of Burda Patterns, Inc., Marietta, GA.

	Vogue #1002 and #2926	McCall's #6985	Simplicity #8239	Style #2712	Burda #3752
Waist (Body)	25" (63.5 cm)	25" (63.5 cm)	25" (63.5 cm)	25" (63.5 cm)	26" (66 cm)
Waistband	$26^{1}/8$" (66.25 cm)	$26^{1}/2$" (67.5 cm)	$26^{1}/4$" (66.5 cm)	$25^{7}/8$" (65.75 cm)	$26^{3}/4$" (68 cm)
Waistband Ease	$1^{1}/8$" (2.75 cm)	$1^{1}/2$" (4 cm)	$1^{1}/4$" (3.2 cm)	$^{7}/8$" (2.2 cm)	$^{3}/4$" (2 cm)
Waist of Pant (Pattern)	$26^{1}/2$" (67.5)	$26^{3}/4$" (68 cm)	$27^{1}/2$" (70 cm)	$27^{3}/4$" (70.5 cm)	$27^{1}/4$" (69 cm)
Waist Ease	$1^{1}/2$" (4 cm)	$1^{3}/4$" (4.5 cm)	$2^{1}/2$" (6.5 cm)	$2^{3}/4$" (7 cm)	$2^{1}/4$" (5.75 cm)
Low Hip (Body)	$34^{1}/2$" (87.5 cm)	$34^{1}/2$" (87.5 cm)	$34^{1}/2$" (87.5 cm)	$34^{1}/2$" (87.5 cm)	$35^{1}/2$" (90 cm)
Low Hip (Pattern)	$38^{3}/4$" (98.5 cm)	$37^{3}/4$" (96 cm)	39" (99 cm)	$40^{1}/2$" (103 cm)	$39^{1}/4$" (99.5 cm)
Low Hip Ease	$4^{1}/4$" (11 cm)	$3^{1}/4$" (8.5 cm)	$4^{1}/2$" (14 cm)	6" (15 cm)	$3^{3}/4$" (9.5 cm)
Front High Hip	$16^{1}/2$" (42 cm)	$16^{1}/2$" (42 cm)	$15^{1}/2$" (39.5 cm)	$17^{3}/4$" (45 cm)	$16^{1}/2$" (42 cm)
Back Low Hip	21" (53.5 cm)	20" (51 cm)	$20^{1}/2$" (52 cm)	19" (48.5 cm)	$20^{1}/4$" (51.5 cm)
Hip Depth*	$9^{1}/2$" (24 cm)	9" (23 cm)	9" (23 cm)	9" (23 cm)	9" (23 cm)
Front Crotch Length	$11^{7}/8$" (30.25 cm)	$12^{1}/8$" (30.75 cm)	$12^{1}/2$" (31.5 cm)	$10^{3}/4$" (27.5 cm)	$11^{3}/8$" (29 cm)
Back Crotch Length	$14^{1}/2$" (37 cm)	$13^{1}/2$-14" (34-36 cm)	$14^{3}/4$" (37.5 cm)	$14^{1}/4$" (36 cm)	$14^{1}/4$" (36 cm)
Total Crotch Length	$26^{3}/8$" (67 cm)	$25^{5}/8$-$26^{1}/8$" (65-66.25 cm)	$27^{1}/4$" (69 cm)	25" (63.5 cm)	$25^{5}/8$" (65 cm)
Crotch Depth	$11^{1}/2$" (29 cm)	$11^{3}/8$" (28.75 cm)	$11^{1}/2$" (29 cm)	$10^{1}/4$" (26 cm)	$10^{1}/4$" (26 cm)
Inseam	$29^{3}/8$" (74.75 cm)	$29^{3}/4$" (75.5 cm)	$29^{3}/4$" (75.5 cm)	$30^{1}/2$" (77.5 cm)	$27^{1}/2$" (70 cm)
Outseam	$40^{3}/4$" (103.5 cm)	40" (101.5 cm)	$40^{3}/4$" (103.5 cm)	$40^{1}/2$" (103 cm)	$37^{3}/4$" (96 cm)
Front Thigh	$10^{1}/2$" (26.5 cm)	$10^{1}/8$" (25.75 cm)	$11^{3}/4$" (30 cm)	$11^{1}/4$" (28.5 cm)	11" (28 cm)
Back Thigh	$14^{3}/8$" (36.5 cm)	$12^{3}/4$" (32.5 cm)	$14^{3}/4$" (37.5 cm)	$13^{1}/2$" (34.5 cm)	$13^{3}/4$" (35 cm)
Total Thigh	$24^{7}/8$" (63 cm)	$22^{7}/8$" (58.25 cm)	$26^{1}/2$" (67.5 cm)	$24^{3}/4$" (63 cm)	$24^{3}/4$" (63 cm)

* Measured at the fullest point, not necessarily where the hip line is indicated.

As in Chapter Two for the dress fitting patterns, we have charted the different companies' key measurements for these patterns. Note that only Vogue #1002, McCall's #6985, and Burda #3752 were specifically intended to be used as fitting patterns. Simplicity and Style do not provide official pant fitting patterns, and the Vogue pattern may be a special order item in your area. Therefore, for the sake of comparison, we have chosen basic fashion patterns from these companies' current catalogues for relatively narrow-fitted pants with a waistband and waist darts or soft pleats. Any of these could serve as fitting patterns, but because fashion patterns tend to come and go with the seasons and style trends, pattern numbers in the chart may not be the same as those in the later pattern catalogues. A careful review of the catalogues will, however, produce equivalent examples in every year and season.

Note also that all of the patterns have allowed considerably more wearing ease at the waist, at least in the waistline seam of the pant pieces, than do the dress patterns in the preceding chapters. This is because more ease is needed to sit and bend in close-fitting pants than in a skirt. Well-made pants often provide for up to an additional 1 inch (2.5 cm) to be eased into the waistband. Other differences can be noted in the crotch depth and the way in which the crotch length has been distributed between the front and back curves. The Simplicity fashion pattern, in particular, seems to have considerably more fashion ease than the fitting patterns, perhaps because soft pleats have been substituted for the waist darts.

REVIEWING YOUR FIGURE

Remember, back in the first and second chapters, when you and your fitting buddy were scrutinizing your individual shapes? Did you notice whether you carried your weight below your waist evenly or if it was concentrated at the front or the sides? Do your thighs tend to be relatively heavy and, if so, is that weight in the front or at the sides? Were your hips relatively level, or do you have the very common characteristic of one hip higher than the other? When fitting the skirt, did you note if your hip curve was comparatively flat or very curvy, and was the fullest part of that curve high or low?

Take into consideration how you like pants to fit and look again at the pants patterns on the grid. Then, study the comparative measurements in the chart and note those areas where you might be slightly out of proportion. Which company's silhouette seems closest to yours? This does not mean that you must limit yourself to using that brand of patterns. However, you may have to make more adjustments to the other pattern brands to achieve good fit.

TAKING YOUR MEASUREMENTS

Now comes another one of those moments of truth—picking up the tape measure. You can simply transfer to the Pants Measurement Chart on page 84 the following measurements from the Personal Measurement Chart you completed in Chapter Three:

- total waist (#3)
- front waist (#3A)
- back waist (#3B)
- total hip (#4)
- high front hip (#4A)
- low back hip (#4B)
- high hip (#8A)
- hip depth (#8B)

HIP DEPTH

Wear the same leotard and foundation garments you wore for the dress measurements (note that, to measure crotch length, a slip is impractical here) and tie or pin the pieces of narrow elastic around your waist and low hipline. The hip elastic should pass over the fullest back curve but should not be below the crotch in the front. Make sure it is parallel to the ground. Re-attach the plumb line(s) at your side, to determine the natural position for the side seam.

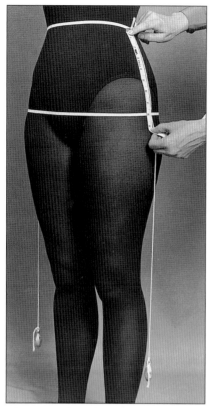

Measuring hip depth, using elastic strips as reference points for waist and low hipline. Plumb line indicates the natural dividing line of the body, for measuring high front hip and low back hip.

CROTCH LENGTH

With your legs slightly apart, your fitting buddy will measure the crotch length (#12): the distance from the crotch point to the center front waistline, and then the distance from the crotch point to the back center waistline. And you thought the dress measurements were embarrassing! It is helpful to join the beginning ends of two tape measures with adhesive tape and place this joint at the crotch point. To help determine both your crotch

point and the location of your inseam, tie a plumb line to the joint of the two tape measures and let it fall between your legs toward your ankles. If you are careful to keep the tapes loose enough for comfort, this process will be less awkward.

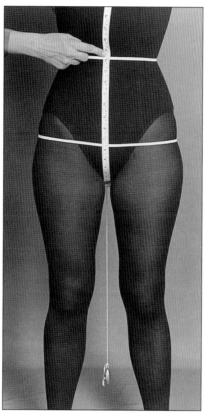

Measuring crotch length with two measuring tapes joined at their beginning ends.

CROTCH DEPTH

There are several approaches to taking the crotch depth measurement (#13). We think the easiest is to sit on a firm surface and have your fitting buddy measure from the side waist point along the outseam line to that surface.

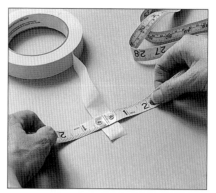

Joining tape measures at their beginning ends, for easier measuring of crotch length.

THIGH MEASUREMENT

Your fitting buddy should measure the circumference of your thigh (#14) at the fullest point, usually right at the crotch line. You might also want to make a note whether there is a need for greater fullness at the front or the sides.

OUTSEAM

Following the natural line indicated by the side plumb line(s), your fitting buddy will measure the outseam (#15): from the side waist point to just below the outside ankle bone. Your ankle may not be where you want your pants to end, especially if you customarily wear high-heeled shoes with pants, but it is a good reference point. If you and your fitting buddy have noted that one of your hips is decidedly higher than the other, you may want to take this measurement on both sides in case they differ.

Pants Measurement Chart

	Body Measurements	Wearing Ease	Total Body Measurements	$1/2$-Total Body Measurements	Pattern Measurements	Changes + or –
	3. Total Waist					
	3A. Front Waist	+1/2" (1.25 cm)				
	3B. Back Waist	+1/2" (1.25 cm)				
	4. Total Hip					
	4A. High Front Hip	+³/₄" (2 cm)				
	4B. Low Back Hip	+1" (2.5 cm)				

Record all measurements in the appropriate box, using a pencil in case revisions are needed later. You may wish to photocopy the charts so that you can use them more than once. NOTE: All body and pattern measurements should be rounded up to the nearest ¹/₈ inch (3mm). The shaded boxes will not be filled in.

	Body Measurements	Wearing Ease	Total Body Measurements	½-Total Body Measurements	Pattern Measurements	Changes + or –
HIP BONE	8A. Waistline to High Hipline	0"				
HIP DEPTH 3"	8B. Hip Depth	0"				
CENTER POINT	12. Crotch Length	0"				
	13. Crotch Depth	0"				
	14. Thigh Circumference	3" (7.5 cm) or more for style				
WAIST TO ANKLE	15. Outseam	0"				

Name _____   Notes:

Date _____

Height _____ Weight _____

Size _____ Pattern Co. _____

Choosing Your Pants Pattern

Your full hip measurement will be the best indication of the proper pant pattern size you should choose. You may be very surprised to learn that your pant size is as much as one or two, or even more, sizes away from your dress size—this is quite normal. Therefore, if you are making a pant suit or pants and top, you may need to buy two different size patterns or a multi-size pattern with the proper range of sizes to fit your individual needs. Please remember that this is no reflection on your personal worth. It simply means that you have your own distinctive body silhouette and proportions, and they must be taken into account when fitting your clothes.

Preparing the Pattern

Just as you did with the dress fitting pattern, rough-cut the pattern, leaving as much extra tissue as possible, and use a barely warm dry iron to smooth away any wrinkles. If you have a multi-size pattern, use a colored pencil or flow pen to mark the proper cutting line for your size. Then use the flexible gridded ruler and the same pen or pencil to draw in all stitching lines (if not already provided), high front and low back hiplines (the hip point is often indicated on patterns with the same symbol used to indicate the bust point), and crotch line. If

you are working with the McCall's pattern, you will notice that extra tissue for lengthening is provided; fold along the lower horizontal lengthen/shorten line, bring it up to the upper line, and tape it in place.

MEASURING THE PATTERN

Consult the Pants Measurement Chart and measure all the corresponding areas on the pattern pieces. Record the results in the "Pattern Measurement" column. If you are using the Simplicity pattern with the soft pleats, fold out the pleats all the way to a point below the crotch line, to get accurate front waist, high hip, and thigh measurements. If you have decided to use a different basic pant pattern than those in the chart on page 81, and the pattern you have chosen includes slant pockets, remember to include the pattern piece for the back of the pocket and match it to all of the appropriate symbols when you measure the waistline, outseam, thigh, and high front hip. If you don't include the pocket back, your pattern piece measurements will not be accurate, so it's a good idea to tape the pocket in place for measurements and fittings. When measuring the back crotch length on the McCall's pattern, use the middle line.

In the final "Changes" column, calculate the adjustment you will have to make in each area to make the pattern conform to your body proportions. Keep in mind all the

points you and your fitting buddy noted about your own unique shape and how ready-to-wear pants tend to fit you. These will offer valuable hints about which corrections you must make to the pattern.

Minor Adjustments to Pants

Perhaps the most common complaint about pants is that the crotch is either uncomfortably loose or too high and tight. Wrinkles and stress lines generally indicate unwanted tightness, and folds indicate too much fullness. The first adjustments to consider, therefore, will be to crotch length (front and back) and crotch depth. Comparing your body measurements to those of the pattern may at first be very confusing. You may find that you need to increase one, such as crotch length, and decrease the other, such as crotch depth, which at first seems impossible. Remember the time-worn principle of physics, that every action causes a reaction? This is especially true in the area of the crotch—lengthening or shortening crotch depth also changes crotch length.

CROTCH DEPTH

Begin your alterations by correcting the crotch depth in both the front and back. The good news is that, if you need a change of 1 inch (2.5 cm) or less in the crotch depth, or if the crotch depth conflicts with apparent changes you need to make in crotch length, you do nothing. You will re-evaluate these areas after the tissue fit. You may discover that other needed changes will also correct the crotch depth problem. This is one of those rare moments in which the action-reaction principle works in your favor. Rejoice and be grateful!

If the needed crotch depth change is between 1 and 2 inches (2.5 and 5 cm) and does not conflict with an apparent crotch length change, alter the pattern in this area by adjusting the lengthen/shorten lines on both the front and back. Cut or fold along the parallel lines and, if necessary, add tissue. See Figure 1. If you think you need an adjustment of more than 2 inches (5 cm), make

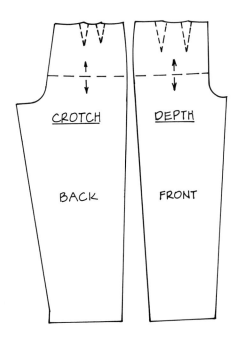

Figure 1. Adjusting crotch depth at lengthen/shorten lines.

half of the adjustment now and test it during the tissue fit.

BACK CROTCH LENGTH

Because we are usually more conscious of discomfort or poor fit in the back, turn your attention there next. Once you have made the crotch depth adjustment, re-measure the back crotch length on the pattern—from crotch point to center back at the waistline—and determine

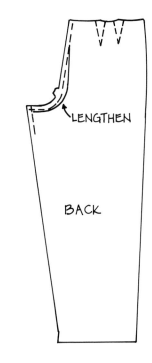

Figure 2. Adjusting back crotch length. In this case, back crotch is lengthened by drawing a deeper curve.

how much additional change you need. Then redraw the crotch curve—less curve to shorten and more curve to lengthen. See Figure 2. For a moderate adjustment, you can shorten by re-curving in to a maxi-

mum of $1/4$ inch (6 mm) inside the original line, or lengthen the curve by drawing a new line $1/2$ inch (1.25 cm) outside the original line. For a larger adjustment, you can re-curve up to 1 inch (2.5 cm) outside the original curve.

Conventional wisdom in the sewing industry has it that the European pattern-makers, especially Burda, have always allowed for more crotch curve. Our comparisons, however, indicate that American companies are catching on, at least in the back curve. The McCall's pattern anticipates this common correction and provides three possible crotch curves. The more significant difference we noted is that the American companies tend to allow for greater crotch depth and for a longer front crotch curve than do their European cousins. Another difference is that the back seam in the Burda pant is more angled in relation to the grainline than in the American patterns, which makes it slightly biased, allowing for greater flexibility.

The deeper back curve, while providing more length, will also eliminate some of the bagginess in the seat area. Some low hip circumference will be lost, but it is usually not significant and can be adjusted for in the side seam. One of us learned this particular action-reaction lesson as a newlywed attempting to adjust the crotch of her husband's ready-to-wear trousers. It is a testament to his willingness to forgive and her ability to learn that the marriage is still alive and well after thirty-two years!

Wedge Adjustment for Back Crotch Length

If, after making the above changes, you still need up to 1 inch (2.5 cm) additional crotch length in the back and you and your fitting buddy have noted that you do not have a particularly prominent seat curve, you may be able to achieve good fit with a wedge adjustment. We do not recommend this alteration for the front. For the back, however, try this adjustment before proceeding to the major alteration—but remember that you cannot use this adjustment for a change of more than 1 inch (2.5 cm) total. The center back seam in virtually every pants pattern functions like a dart, shaping the back curve from waist to hip. The wedge adjustment performed in the back angles this "dart" more acutely, resulting in a much better fit for those who have a relatively small waist and a seat curve that is both low and pronounced, and for those who have a swayback posture. On the other hand, overlapping the wedge compensates for the relatively flat seat common in older figures; it accomplishes this by straightening out and reducing the dart-like angle of the center back seam.

To make the wedge adjustment, follow these steps:

1. Make a horizontal slash through the center back seam allowance and seamline, perpendicular to the grainline, all the way across to, but not through, the side seamline. If you have not already used the lengthen/shorten lines to adjust for crotch depth, make the slash along one of these lines. If you have already used them, draw another horizontal line either a little above or slightly below the lengthen/shorten lines and slash along it.

2. Clip through the side seam allowance, leaving a hinge at the seamline.

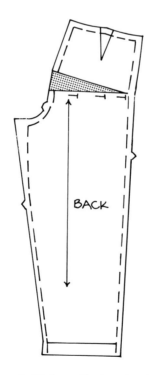

Figure 3. Wedge adjustment, with slashed edges spread apart to lengthen back crotch.

3. If you need to lengthen the crotch, place the pattern over extra tissue on the cork or foam core mat, pin along the lower slash line, and spread the upper piece up to a total of 1 inch (2.5 cm) at the center seamline. See Figure 3.

4. If you need to shorten the crotch to adjust for a flat seat, overlap the two slashed edges up to 1 inch (2.5 cm) at the crotch curve, thus removing a wedge-shaped section of pattern at the center. See Figure 4.

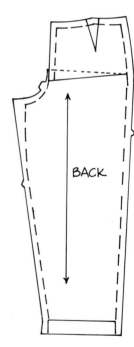

Figure 4. Wedge adjustment, with slashed edges overlapped to shorten back crotch.

5. Blend and true seamline and cutting lines.

If you still need a bit more change in the crotch length, and you and your fitting buddy agree that you need more width in the thigh than has been provided, lengthen the crotch extension slightly, up to 1 inch (2.5 cm). If you need less length and have thin thighs, you may be able to shorten the extension slightly, again up to 1 inch (2.5 cm). See Figure 5. Begin with a $1/2$-inch (1.25-cm) change for the tissue fit. After any change to the crotch extension, blend the inseam and cutting lines to the knee area.

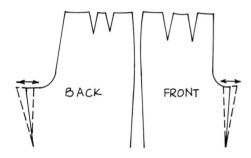

Figure 5. Lengthening or shortening crotch length by adding to or subtracting from crotch extensions.

You will need to re-evaluate this area after the tissue fit since the interrelationship of crotch length, crotch curve, crotch depth, and thigh width is so complex. Your goal is to achieve a smooth comfortable fit, with no points of undue stress and no wrinkles or folds. (Horizontal wrinkles indicate tightness and vertical ones indicate shortness; vertical folds indicate excess width and horizontal folds indicate excess length.) If you cannot make the needed adjustments in back crotch length using the wedge

method, you will need to consider the major adjustment described below.

FRONT CROTCH LENGTH

Once you have made the needed back adjustment, turn your attention to the front crotch length. If a crotch depth change was made, re-measure the front crotch length. If you need further adjustment, there are three methods to do so. First, you can either raise or lower the waistline up to $1/2$ inch (1.25 cm), as you did on the skirt. Second, you can add or subtract from the crotch point; begin with a $1/2$-inch (1.25-cm) correction and re-fit. Third, you can make the same major abdominal correction as you did on the skirt.

NOTE: The front crotch curve is rarely re-curved. However, slight bagginess in front can be eliminated by deepening the curve up to $1/4$ inch (6 mm) or less. It is best to wait until after the tissue or muslin fitting to see if this correction is really necessary. It is better to eliminate any such bagginess by reducing width at the crotch point.

MAJOR ADJUSTMENTS TO PANTS
ADJUSTING FOR CURVY ABDOMEN OR SEAT

By now, you and your fitting buddy have probably noted whether you have an especially prominent curve in the seat or the abdomen. To correct for either curve, use the

major correction for abdomen and seat curves described in Chapter Seven. Choose this alteration if you do not have a swayback and the line from your waist to the hip is relatively straight but full. To review:

1. Draw a line down the center of each waist dart to the dart point. In the front, if there are two darts, use only the one closest to the side seam.

2. Draw a horizontal slash line perpendicular to the grainline from the center front or center back to the closest dart point, and continue this line to the next dart point. Note that the second portion of this line may not be perpendicular to the grainline if the second dart is a different length than the first.

3. Continue the line at a diagonal from the second dart point up to the side waist point. See Figure 6.

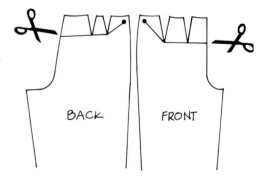

Figure 6. Slash lines for major curve adjustment.

4. Slash along this line to the waist point and create a hinge by clipping through the seam allowance.

5. Slash down the center of each dart to create a hinge at each dart point.

6. To add crotch length and hip width, carefully place the pattern piece on top of extra tissue on the cork or foam core mat; pin at the waist point hinge and along the lower edge of the slash.

7. Gently spread the edges apart the desired distance at the center front or back. See Figure 7. The maximum addition you can make is 1 inch (2.5 cm) to the front and 2 inches (5 cm) to the back. A rectangle will form below the darts, a wedge will form toward the side seam, and the darts will open up.

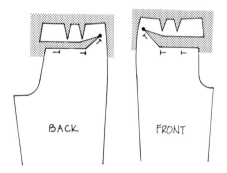

Figure 7. Adjusting for curvy abdomen in front and curvy seat in back.

8. Pin and tape everything firmly in place; redraw the center seamline and cutting lines or the zipper extension.

NOTE: It is important that the center front seamline remain parallel to the grainline. Otherwise, it will not lie properly over the abdomen. To keep the center front seamline parallel to the grainline, the waistline may

actually become smaller. Therefore, make any further adjustments at the darts or side seam to maintain needed waist circumference.

ADJUSTING WAIST CIRCUMFERENCE

Once the crotch depth, curve, and length in both the front and back have been corrected, then you can make needed circumference changes, including the relatively minor adjustments of side seams and waist darts. Re-measure the front and back waistlines and high and low hiplines to determine if you need to add or subtract width at any of these points. See Figure 8. As you did in the skirt, you can add up to 1 inch (2.5 cm) at the side seam for additional width at the waist or hip. If you are making corrections in both areas, you may add or subtract more, so long as there is no more than 1 inch (2.5 cm) difference between the two corrections. For example, if you have added 1 inch (2.5 cm) at the waist, you may add up to 2 inches (5 cm) at

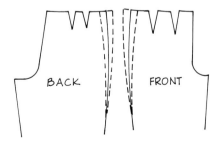

Figure 8. Adjusting waist circumference by adding to or subtracting from side seams.

the hip. To make any greater changes, use the interior width adjustment described below. Once any changes have been made at the side seams, blend and redraw seamlines and cutting lines to the original hemline.

The waist circumference can also be adjusted slightly by either widening or narrowing the darts. However, try not to widen a dart by more than a total of $1/2$ inch (1.25 cm) or it may poke out when sewn. To prevent this poking, a single dart can be divided into two smaller darts or you can curve the darts, using the Fashion Ruler or hip curve to follow the contours of the body where the dart ends become narrower. See Figure 9. If dart corrections, along with side seam adjustments, are insufficient, you will have to consider the interior change below.

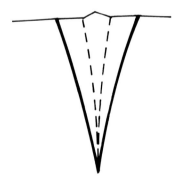

Figure 9. Adjusting waist circumference by making darts wider or narrower.

INTERIOR WIDTH ADJUSTMENTS

Adding or subtracting width to pants—over and above what can be accomplished through the major correction and side seam and dart corrections described above—can be accomplished through interior alteration. This alteration actually involves four areas—waist circumference, hip, thigh, and hem. Interior alteration is effective when used to compensate for a large front thigh, because the adjustment is balanced throughout the front leg and therefore does not over-emphasize the thigh and hip.

To calculate how much alteration is needed, check your waist and hip measurements. Subtract the smaller measurement from the larger to determine how much to accomplish with the interior alteration. For example, if you need to add 2 inches (5 cm) at the waist and 1 inch (2.5 cm) at the hip, make a 1-inch (2.5-cm) interior alteration in both areas and add the remaining 1-inch (2.5-cm) waist correction at the side seam.

Although considered major, the interior alteration is relatively simple and is similar to the procedure you followed on the skirt. Follow these steps:

1. Just outside the waist dart nearest the side seam, measure and draw a slash line parallel to the grainline and extend it the entire length of the pattern piece you are adjusting.

2. Draw a guideline at right angles to the slash line.

3. Cut along the slash line through all seam allowances.

4. Spread apart and insert tissue the needed amount to increase width or overlap to decrease width. See Figure 10. Whether you spread apart or overlap, be sure to keep the cut edges parallel to one another and line up the guideline.

5. Pin and tape in place.

6. Re-measure the waist, hip, and thigh and make any needed adjustments. NOTE: The interior alteration does change the taper of the lower leg, but it does so while retaining the proportion necessary for that pattern piece.

LENGTHENING/SHORTENING

After making all other adjustments, compare your outseam measurements to those of the corrected pattern and make any needed corrections at the lengthen/shorten lines on the leg. If no line is indicated, draw one perpendicular to the grainline just below the knee area, running all the way across from inseam to outseam. See Figure 11. As you have with other pattern pieces, cut or fold along the line or lines, and overlap or spread apart over tissue to make the needed changes. It is best not to make length adjustments at the hemline because it will change the taper of the leg.

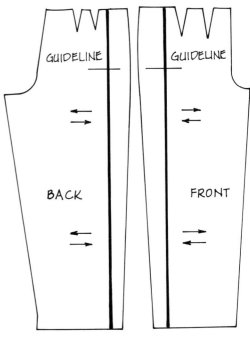

Figure 10. Even interior alteration to add or subtract width.

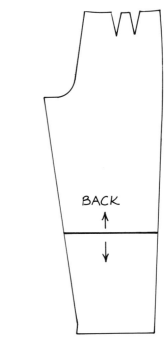

Figure 11. Adjusting for length at lengthen/shorten lines, rather than hemline; this prevents changing the taper of the pant leg.

You have probably noticed that we have yet to change one of the pattern pieces—the waistband. Because this is the easiest piece to adjust and its alteration depends on the final waist dimensions of the pants, adjustments can wait until after the tissue and muslin fits.

THE TISSUE FIT

When all needed corrections have been made, you are ready for the tissue fit, during which you may find that further alterations are required. As you did with the various sections of the dress, be sure that all changes are firmly and smoothly held in place by removable tape. Redraw stitching lines and make 1-inch (2.5-cm) seam allowances at waist, side seam, and inseam; keep crotch seam allowance at $^5/_8$ inch (16 mm). Double-check that each piece lies absolutely flat and that there are no tiny tucks,

wrinkles, or gaps to distort the line of the garment. If need be, use a barely warm dry iron and pressing cloth to re-iron the pattern pieces, working on the wrong side, away from the tape.

After pressing the tissue, tape the crotch curves in front and back to reduce stress during fitting. Place the tape adjacent to the seamline and clip the curve to the stitching line at intervals of about $^1/_2$ inch (1.25 cm). Using the method described on page 57, fold and pin all darts closed, being careful to point all pins away from the waistline, where they might poke the wearer during the tissue fit. Turn up and pin the hem. Finally, turning all seam allowances to the outside for ease of adjustment, pin the side seam and inseam closed, again being careful to point the pins away from sensitive areas.

For the tissue fit you should wear the foundation garments you would normally wear under fitted pants. Reposition the waist and low hip elastic strips, both as a visual guide and base onto which you can pin the pattern pieces. Gently put the half-pant on your right leg. If you and your fitting buddy have noted that you are markedly asym-

metrical from side to side, especially if one hip is higher than the other, after fitting the right leg, re-pin the pattern pieces for the left leg and re-fit it, making all markings and corrections for the left leg in a different color pen or pencil.

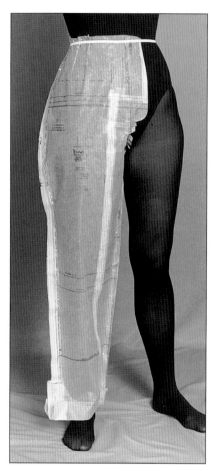

The tissue fit in progress. Bridget, a dancer, needed additional width at the front thigh to fit her well-developed muscles.

Checkpoints

• Areas of special concern to examine during the tissue fit include the curve and fit of the waistline, presence of a swayback, fit of the crotch

Taping crotch curves to reduce stress on the pattern tissue during the tissue fit.

line (front and back), shape of the hip curve (or, in the case of uneven hips, curves), fit of the crotch point and thighs (both front and back, especially at the center), fit over the abdomen and seat curve, and length. Typically, the area causing the greatest concern will be the interrelationship among the crotch curve, crotch depth, and crotch point. All of these, especially the crotch curve, have been affected by any adjustments you made to accommodate your individual front and back curves. Signs of fitting problems are wrinkles or stress lines. It may be necessary to take the tissue off several times, readjust it, and try it on again.

• Check that adjusted darts do not poke out.

• Check the crotch depth and major changes to abdomen or seat to see if they are enough or too much.

• Look at the back crotch curve and inner thigh. If necessary, deepen the crotch curve to correct for a baggy seat.

• Take a final look at the pants leg(s) and length, and note whether the inseam and/or outseam can be reshaped to give a better appearance.

ADJUSTING FOR FRONT THIGH

If you notice excessive tightness in the front thigh area, a fitting problem found in young athletes with highly developed thigh muscles, perform the following L-slash alteration:

1. Draw a vertical line from the hem up the center of the front pant leg to a point opposite and just below the bottom of the fly; take care to keep this line parallel to the grainline.

2. Square a line to the front crotch, just below the fly.

3. Cut up through the hem, along both lines, and through the seam allowance.

4. Place the pattern over tissue and make an even internal correction by spreading the two vertical cut edges up to $^1/_2$ inch (1.25 cm) apart, keeping the cut edges parallel. See Figure 12.

5. Tape in place; blend and redraw the front crotch line.

This alteration, which is a varia-

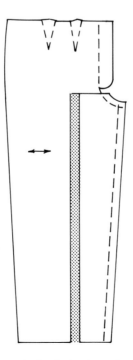

Figure 12. L-slash alteration to add width at front thigh.

tion on the more common full interior correction we have already discussed, relieves the tightness across the front of the thighs without causing the pant leg to gap at the hip or side seams. Note that it is appropriate only for a relatively slender individual with well-developed thighs.

The characteristics of the tissue will make it difficult to anticipate all needed adjustments at this stage. Do not try to sit or bend—the tissue is far too fragile. Sitting and bending in pants will not be tested until the very end of the final muslin fit, since even the relatively stable and rigid muslin may stretch and deceive you as to the actual fit. When you are satisfied that you have adjusted the tissue as much as possible to achieve a good fit, you are ready to begin working with the muslin.

THE MUSLIN

Carefully remove all pins from the tissue and redraw all cutting lines, seamlines, darts, and other pattern guides as needed. At this initial cutting stage, it is wise to leave 1-inch (2.5-cm) seam allowances at the waist, inseam, and side seams. If need be, re-iron the tissue, carefully avoiding the tape. Note that the pockets will not be sewn in the muslin. Therefore, for slant pockets, leave the pocket pattern pieces taped in place when you cut the muslin.

Prepare the pre-washed muslin for layout. Pin the selvages together, making certain that the grain is true. Lay out the back and front pants pieces as directed by the pattern. If you have discovered that one hip is very different from the other, cut each leg piece separately. If the difference between the two sides is very dramatic, you may wish to use extra tissue to make separate front and back pattern pieces for the left leg; tissue-fit this new pattern to be sure that you have accurately transferred all cor-rections and markings. You will wait until after the initial muslin fit to adjust and cut the waistband.

Cut out the muslin and transfer all seamlines and other pattern markings to the wrong side. Set your sewing machine to a longer-than-normal stitch, as you did for the dress muslin. Next, sew the darts, the inseam, and the crotch seam either to within 8 inches (20.5 cm) of the back waist or to the bot-tom of the fly if there is one. Do not back-stitch at the beginning and end of seamlines. Be careful to follow your markings exactly. Clip crotch curves to $1/4$ inch (6 mm) from the seamline. Press all darts toward the center and press open all seam allowances. Press and pin up the hems in the pant legs.

Wearing the proper foundation garments, turn the seam allowances to the inside and try on the muslin. Carefully assess all the potential problem areas. Since the muslin is much softer than the tissue, it is not unusual for wrinkles to appear at this stage that you did not notice during the tissue fit.

Checkpoints

• Evaluate all areas where there are prominent curves—abdomen, rear, thighs, and calves.

• Be especially careful to note the fit of the crotch line.

• Note the fit of the pant legs in the area of the crotch point, especially if you have made any adjustments in the length of the crotch extensions by moving the crotch point. The European pattern companies design their pants to have a slightly higher crotch point, fitting somewhat closer to the body, but even these should not be tight or binding.

• Check also that the hip curve of the pants matches yours. This is especially important if you like set-in pockets in your pants. If the garment is too tight or your hip curve is higher or more prominent than the curve of the pants, you

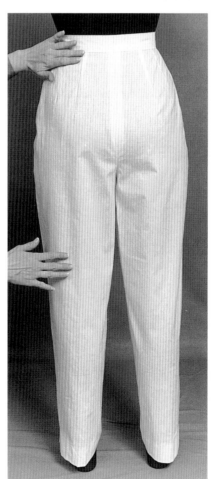

The muslin fit in progress.

will have unattractive gaps and bulges at the pockets.

Re-read our definition of good fit on page 7. Do your pants now qualify? If not, make the needed adjustments and be sure to transfer all changes to the tissue. Re-stitch and try on the pants as many times as needed to achieve a good fit. When you are satisfied that these are the most perfectly fitting pants you have ever worn, you are ready for the final touch—the waistband.

THE WAISTBAND

After transferring any changes made during the muslin fit to the pattern, create the waistband by first measuring the waist seamline of the pants tissue. Now measure the length of the waistband provided by the pattern company for your size. To allow for comfort, the waistband should be approximately 1 inch (2.5 cm) larger than your body measurement, and the waist seamline of the pants should be 1 inch (2.5 cm) larger than the waistband. This will allow for ease over the curves of your body and will give you some breathing and eating room. Determine what the total waistband measurement should be, **excluding the extensions for fasteners**, and compare to the waist measurement of the pants.

If the pants waistline needs adjusting to accommodate for necessary ease, make the corrections at the side seams or the darts. If the

original waistband needs alteration, measure the correct waist seam for the front and back separately, using the pants waistline as a guide. Subtract $1/4$ inch (6 mm) from each quarter-section of the pant waistline to arrive at the proper length for the corresponding section of the waistband. Before proceeding, double-check the total length of the waistband.

Lay out and cut the waistband. Transfer all markings, including the side waist points. Fold in half lengthwise and press. With right sides together, baste the waistband to the pants, matching side seam and center markings, easing as needed. Turn the waistband up and press. Try on the muslin pants one more time to check the fit. If you are satisfied, you can now test it in the sitting and bending positions.

If the back of the waistline seems to move down a bit when you bend or sit, do not be concerned. This is perfectly natural in all pants, except those made of stretch fabrics. If it pulls down further than you would like, add a little to the back at the waistline or try an additional wedge correction in the back.

NOTE: When you use your fitting pattern to make pants out of fabrics heavier than muslin, sew a $1/2$-inch (1.25-cm) side seam allowance rather than the conventional $5/8$ inch (16 mm) to compensate for the heavier fabric; do the same for pants you intend to line. An alternative is

to adjust the side seam and cutting lines to provide an extra $1/8$ inch (3 mm) of width. You may also wish to vary the length of the hem, depending on the types of shoes you will wear with the pants.

Chapter Nine

Preserving and using your personal fitting patterns

After many hours of self-scrutiny and meticulous work, you are now the proud owner of personal fitting patterns for both a basic dress and pants. You probably are questioning their value. How will you use them? Will you have to go through this entire complicated process every time you sew a new fashion pattern? What good is a fitted dress pattern and narrow pants when you prefer clothes with a more relaxed fit?

Your personal fitting patterns can be considered a kind of recipe. Regardless of the style or manufacturer of the specific fashion pattern you choose, you now know the dimensions you need to achieve the best fit and how to adjust any pattern to match these dimensions. Many styles will allow more design ease than your fitting pattern provides, but you now know that this ease must be **in addition** to the minimum fitting ease your fitting pattern allows.

The first step in using your fitting patterns is to preserve them. Your instinct might be simply to transfer the finished pattern to a fresh piece of tissue or to one of the non-woven interfacing fabrics also sold as a long-lasting tissue substitute. The problem with acting on this impulse, however, is that you will no longer have a visual record of how you arrived at these dimensions.

Instead, we recommend that you mount and preserve your finished personal patterns, complete with colored markings and tissue inserts, onto non-woven interfacing, freezer paper, or, if you prefer a rigid master pattern, onto poster board. Your original tissue can be fused to the poster board by using one of the fusible webs on the market. To apply the tissue to poster board, cut a piece of fusible web the size of the tissue pattern. Place tissue face down on the ironing board and lay the fusible web, rough side down, onto the back of the tissue. If there is a paper coating on the web, this should be on top; in this case, follow the manufacturer's directions to fuse the web

Basic Fitting Terms

Review the following terms from Chapter Eight: CULOTTES, PALAZZO PANTS, PANTS, and TROUSERS.

A-LINE. A semi-fitted dress style that is fairly closely-fitted at the bust, then flares out in a more relaxed fit over the waist and hips to a semi-full hemline.

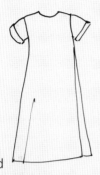

BASQUE WAIST. An elongated fitted bodice, with princess seaming, that ends in the vicinity of the high hipline; very flattering to most figures and especially common in wedding gowns.

CARDIGAN JACKET. A semi-fitted collarless jacket, fitted to the bust and then falling straight to a point near the high hip.

CHEMISE OR TENT. A full dress falling from the shoulders with little or no shaping below the bust. The chemise tends to be straighter and the tent more flared.

DOLMAN SLEEVE. Adapted from the loose fit of folk garments such as the Turkish tunic, a sleeve that is

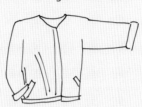

wide and square and is part of the bodice, rather than a separate piece to be set in.

FUSIBLE WEB. A non-woven web of adhesive, usually packaged with one smooth side (or sometimes with paper on one side) that melts and adheres to fabric or other material when heat and steam are applied. It is sold in various widths and several weights under brand names such as Wonder Under, Stitch Witchery, and Heat 'n Bond. Fusible web is right up there with removable tape as a major accomplishment of the twentieth century!

GORED SKIRT. A gore is another name for a seam. In a gored skirt, four or more flared sections are joined to create a skirt that is semi-fitted to the high hipline and increasingly full below.

PRINCESS SEAM. A popular style of bodice in which vertical seams extend from the shoulder seam or, more commonly, the armhole. Princess seams substitute for the front bust and waist darts and back shoulder and waist darts. The side front and side back pieces are eased to the curving seamline, to accommodate the curves of the bust and shoulder blades. Frequently the seamlines extend all the way to the full hemline.

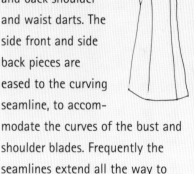

RAGLAN SLEEVES. Loose-fitting sleeves that are set into the bodice with diagonal seams from the neckline to the armhole.

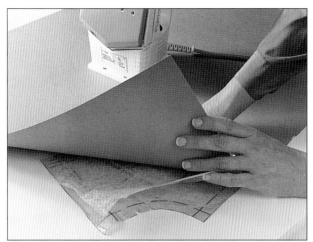

Preserving the personal fitting pattern by fusing the pieces to poster board with a fusible web.

to the tissue and peel the paper away. Next, or if there is no paper, iron the uncut poster board and, while it is still hot, place it on top of the web. Turn the three layers so that the tissue side is up and, using a pressing cloth to protect the tape and your iron, continue fusing. Trim away the excess poster board.

If you decide to mount your pattern on freezer paper, you will find that one side of the paper acts much like a fusible web when ironed. There are also fusible interfacings on the market, which will make the mounting process much easier. When using any fusible product, follow the manufacturer's instructions and be sure to protect your pattern tissue with a pressing cloth.

Once your pattern is mounted, you will be able to see at a glance the precise changes you made. You can then quickly and easily transfer these changes to any fashion pattern that is the same size and preferably, but not necessarily, from the same manufacturer. If you are comfortable with adding your own seam allowances as you cut out the fashion fabric, you may wish to cut these away on your pattern when you mount it. If you do so, however, be sure to mark all notches and other sewing marks. The absence of seam allowances makes it easier to accurately compare the basic pattern pieces to the fashion pattern pieces.

USING YOUR FITTING PATTERN WITH FASHION PATTERNS

What if, in the process of developing your fitting pattern, you have discovered that many of your favorite fashion patterns are the wrong size? Do not despair! The techniques you have learned in altering your fitting pattern will enable you to make the needed changes so that your fashion patterns will match your fitting patterns. If your patterns are just one size smaller or larger than your fitting pattern, you can simply make the needed corrections more or less generous, keeping the proportions the same. You may also want to mount your favorite fashion patterns on a more permanent material once you have made the appropriate fitting changes.

When you begin to work with fashion patterns, use your fitting pattern as a guide. The alterations that you will **always** have to make are the bust cup and shoulder changes for the bodice; the prominent curve changes (front and back) for the bodice, skirt, and pants; and additional changes of crotch depth and crotch length in pants. Other alterations that are frequently needed are the lengthening and shortening of various pattern pieces and, occasionally, circumference additions or subtractions.

Even if the fashion pattern is from a different company than your basic pattern, you can use your fitting pattern as a tool to determine what changes you must make. To determine alterations for the bodice, place the center lines of the fronts and backs on top of the fashion pattern bodice, matching seamlines with fold lines, and match the shoulder and neck points as closely as you can. For the sleeve, match the centers of the sleeve, usually marked by the grainline symbol, and the bicep level. For the skirt, match the center seamlines or fold lines and the waistline at the center front and back. Pants often present a more difficult challenge. As best you can, match the centers at the waist. In some cases, the grainlines will be parallel to one another, but not always.

Once you have matched the key points, look to see how the two patterns compare in the following areas: angle of the shoulder; depth of the neck; width of the chest and back, and of the bust, hips, and bicep; lengths of bodice front and back; lengths of skirt, pants, and sleeve; crotch depth and length; crotch curve; and leg shape. A further comparison to make is between the bust, waist, hip, and length measurements listed on the pattern envelope and the actual measurements of these areas on the fashion pattern. If you subtract the fitting ease for each of these areas, as indicated on the Measurement Charts, you will determine how much design ease has been built in. Finally, compare your own body measurements plus fitting ease to the dimensions of the pattern, to be sure you have the same amount of design ease. If not, you may have to make adjustments, just as you did in the previous chapters. Use your basic pattern as a guide.

If the garment you are making is very loose-fitting—full palazzo pants or an oversized shirt, for example—you may decide that you do not need to make bust cup or other changes that provide more room for pronounced curves. However, be sure that enough design ease will

remain to preserve the look the designer intended. Whenever you are in doubt, tissue-fit or make a muslin before you cut the fashion fabric. You do not want to make any expensive mistakes!

ALTERING A FITTED FASHION PATTERN

Greater difficulties are presented in a close-fitting garment with princess seaming, such as a wedding gown or tailored jacket. Princess seaming is popular for fitted garments because it is more easily adjusted to accommodate individual curves. The princess curve acts much like the side dart in the bodice of your fitting pattern. The point at which the most pronounced curve

turns downward is the bust point, and it may or may not be in the correct place for you. See Figure 1. Use your fitting pattern to determine the correct bust point and indicate it on the fashion pattern.

BUST CUP ALTERATION

If you need to make a bust cup alteration, follow these steps:

1. At the level of the corrected bust point on the center front panel, draw a horizontal line from the center front through the side front seam.

2. Slash and spread over tissue, lengthening the front just as you did your fitting pattern.

3. Pin and tape everything securely in place. See Figure 2.

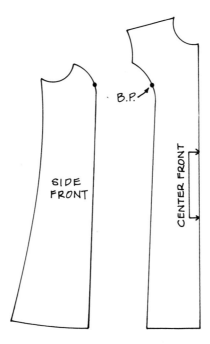

Figure 1. Locating the bust point on the side front and center front pieces of a princess style pattern.

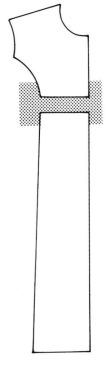

Figure 2. Beginning the bust cup alteration on a princess style pattern by slashing and spreading the center front at the level of the bust point.

4. Compare the original bust point on the pattern to the curved side seam on the center front panel. Is this bust point on the seamline or some distance away? Does the curved seam on the center front panel need to be moved out for your bust point to keep the same distance relationship as the original? If so, adjust the seam and continue the change all the way down to the hem.

5. Blend the new seamline you have created up into the curved princess seam or to the straight line of the shoulder princess seam.

To continue the bust cup alteration on the side panel, follow these steps:

1. Locate the new bust point level and draw a horizontal line from the curved edge of the side front seam through the side seam.

2. Slash from the curved edge to the side seamline; clip the seam allowance to create a hinge.

3. Spread apart over tissue the same amount at the curved seam as you did for the center front panel. See Figure 3.

4. Pin and tape in place.

You have just completed the bust cup alteration for length and have probably also added a bit of width at the curved seam of the center front panel. Now you must make the correction to add the needed amount of extra width. Check your fitting pattern to find the amount you added at the center of the waist

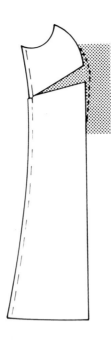

Figure 3. Continuing the bust cup alteration on a princess style pattern by slashing and spreading the side front piece at the level of the bust point.

dart. This amount is usually added to the curved seam of the side front. If, however, there was an addition at the curved seam of the front, then add only the difference to the side panel seam. Measure out from the bust level of the side panel and make a mark. Blend up to the curve or straight line of the princess seam, as needed, and continue down to the hemline, adding the same amount. Note that you have now added to the circumference of both the waist and hips. If you do not need this width, blend the seam and cutting lines, starting from the bust level, back into the original lines at the waist and hip levels.

Your bust cup correction is now complete.

If you need to make a bust correction for an A cup size, follow the above procedure in reverse, overlapping the wedge at the side panel

rather than spreading it apart. Use the measurements from your fitting pattern as a guide and, as always, test with a tissue fit.

Checkpoints

• Check that the curved or straight seams are the same length. If there is a difference, the side panel can be up to $1/2$ inch (1.25 cm) longer, for easing in the bust area. If the side panel is now too short, add to the curve or make the wedge wider; a tissue fit will help you decide which addition to do.

You may be able to predict any needed change by measuring the corrected pattern and comparing it to measurement #2A on the Personal Measurement Chart. If you plan to make an L-slash shoulder alteration, delay making any further correction until the L-slash is completed, since it may also affect the bust area.

NECKLINE GAPPING

While you are still working with the front of the princess bodice, you may need an adjustment to eliminate neckline "gaposis," or gapping at the neckline. This problem will usually be solved by the bust cup alteration and proper sewing techniques. If after doing a tissue fit, however, you find the neckline gapping, try the following solution and check it with a tissue fit:

1. On the center front panel, locate the bust point and draw a diagonal line from the neckline edge through the bust point to the curved front stitching lines.

2. Slash along this line from the neckline and clip the seam allowance to create a hinge at the side front seamline.

3. Overlap the slashed edges up to ½ inch (1.25 cm) at the neckline. See Figure 4.

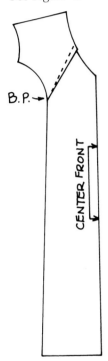

Figure 4. Slashing and overlapping the center front of a princess style pattern to eliminate neckline gapping.

The neckline will now be shorter and will hug the body more closely. This correction can be made only to a bust dart or a princess-line side front seam. Remember to make the identical correction to the front neck facing.

ADJUSTMENTS FOR UPPER BACK CURVE

A prominent curve alteration can also be done in the upper back of

the princess style, in the same manner as the bust correction, except that the alteration is higher up along the back center panel and extends into the armhole. Use your fitting pattern as a guide to determine where to draw the slash lines. In the center back panel, draw a slightly diagonal line from the horizontal slash up to the center of the shoulder seam. Cut across the horizontal line to the shoulder point, creating a hinge by clipping through the seam allowance. Slash down along the diagonal line, leaving a hinge above the horizontal cut. See Figure 5. When the pieces are spread, a dart will form at the shoulder. This may be sewn as a dart or eased into the shoulder seam.

If there is too much fullness to be eased, you can subtract up to

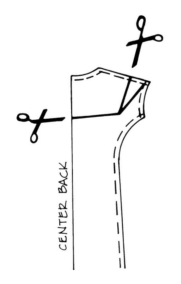

Figure 5. Slash lines for upper back curve alteration on a curved-to-armhole princess style.

⅜ inch (1 cm) at the end of the shoulder seam on the back panel. Tissue-fit to determine if more width is required. If it is, add up to ¼ inch (6 mm) of this width at the side panel curved seams. An additional ⅜ inch (1 cm) could be added at the center back by creating a curved seam there to replace the straight seam or center fold. If you are working with the straight princess line, the back alteration slash and spread lines are very similar to those in front. When adding width, follow the above instructions to alter the center back and side back seams. See Figure 6.

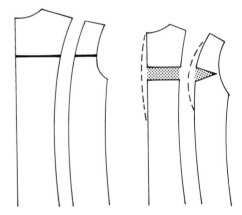

Figure 6. Upper back alteration on a straight-to-shoulder princess style.

PRINCESS SHOULDER CORRECTION

After you have completed the major alterations for prominent front and back curves, move on to the shoulders. If you have a curved-to-the-armhole princess seam, you may need to make a shoulder correction. If this is the case, make a modified L-correction, following these steps:

1. On the side panel, draw a horizontal line from the armhole notches to the curved seam and a perpendicular guideline in the middle of the panel. See Figure 7.

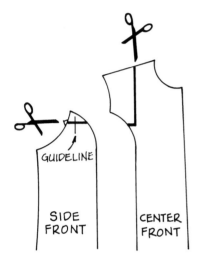

Figure 7. Cutting lines for L-slash alteration on a curved-to-armhole princess style to lengthen or shorten shoulder seam.

2. In the center panel, draw an L-slash line from the shoulder to about where the horizontal slash in the side panel would intersect the curved seam.

3. Cut the L-slash on the center panel, add tissue if needed, and draw the alteration line.

4. Match the slash line to the alteration line; pin and tape in place.

5. On the side panel, slash along the horizontal line and add tissue if needed; draw an alteration line to

make the same correction as you made to the center panel. See Figure 8.

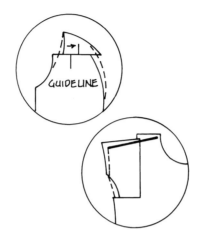

Figure 8. Blending seamline after making L-slash alteration to adjust shoulder length.

6. Match the slash line and guideline to the horizontal alteration line and slide the pattern to the alteration line; pin and tape in place.

7. Blend the new seamlines; the shoulder seam should be a straight line.

8. If you are also making the bust cup correction, the side panel can give you more width. In this case, instead of blending the new seamline, blend the entire alteration to below the bust or to the waist, as needed.

If you need to use the wedge correction to shorten or lengthen the shoulder seamline, do so on the center front and back panels of the curved princess line pattern:

1. Draw a diagonal line in from the shoulder seam into the armhole seamline. See Figure 9.

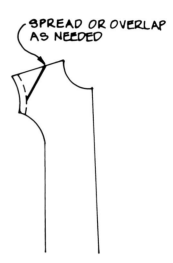

Figure 9. Wedge slash and pivot alteration to adjust shoulder length on a curved-to-armhole princess style.

2. Slash down from the shoulder cutting line and create a hinge at the armhole seamline by clipping the seam allowance.

3. Make the needed correction. If you are doing the straight princess seam, the alteration to shorten the shoulder is made at the side front seams. Take out equal amounts at both sides of the seam to achieve the total correction

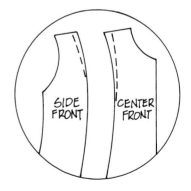

Figure 10. Adjusting shoulder length at side front seams of a straight-to-shoulder princess style.

needed. If you need to take out more in the chest, blend it out of the seam, moving down to the bust. See Figure 10. To complete the princess line pattern, make any other shoulder corrections, side seam additions/subtractions, and any other adjustments to the neckline and lengths as you did on your fitting pattern.

NO-DART BODICE OR DRESS

Loose-fitting dartless garments are designed for those with a B cup or smaller, but women with more prominent curves require a bust dart for shaping. Altering the fashion pattern for a loose-fitting bodice with no darts is similar to what you did on the fitting pattern. For the bust cup alteration, begin finding your bust point by placing the fitting pattern on top of the fashion pattern as described above. Then, draw a line up from the hem to the bust point, parallel to the grainline. From the bust point, draw a diagonal line to the armhole. Look familiar? It is like the one you drew on the fitting pattern bodice to make the bust cup correction. Next, draw a horizontal line from the center front through the bust point to the side seamline. Now, gather up your courage and slash all the way up from the hemline to the bust point and on to, but not through, the armhole seamline. Create a hinge by clipping the seam allowance. Then,

slash along the horizontal line from the side seam to the bust point, creating a second hinge. Spread open as you did on your fitting pattern, to create a bust dart at the side seam. See Figure 11.

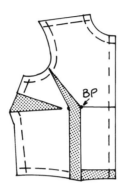

Figure 11. Bust cup alteration for better fit of a loose-fitting dartless garment.

To complete the alteration, redraw the side dart. Before making these corrections, you established the bust point. Part of it remains on the center front pattern piece. Draw a new mid-line for the bust dart from the base of the dart out to the bust point. Establish the end of the dart 1 to 1½ inches (2.5 to 4 cm) away

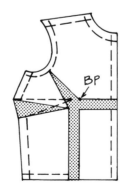

Figure 12. Drawing new bust dart on the previously dartless bodice.

from the bust point toward the side seam along the mid-line and make a dot. This indicates the new bust dart point. Redraw the dart legs from the dart point to the side seam, using the points at which your slashed edges intersect the side seamline as the new dart base. See Figure 12.

Make a horizontal slash from the center front to the bust point and spread the edges apart to re-align the hemline, thus adding the extra length your generous curves require. Your formerly dartless garment will now hang properly—a most desirable result for the small price of having a dart. After completing this correction, make any other changes needed to make the garment fit you.

BUST CUP CORRECTION ON RAGLAN AND DOLMAN STYLES

Bodice styles with raglan and dolman sleeves usually need fewer alterations because of their fullness. Even so, the bust cup and shoulder alterations should be considered. The raglan sleeve bust cup alteration is made in the same manner as on the fitting pattern or dartless bodice described above. Always begin by finding your bust point. If bust and waist darts already exist, make the alteration using those darts, slashing to the armhole notch. See Figure 13. Then, establish your bust point and make any necessary corrections to the dart positions.

The dolman-style bust cup cor-

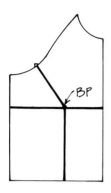

Figure 13. Slash lines for bust cup alteration on the bodice of a raglan style.

rection is also similar to those in the fitting pattern and the dartless bodice, but there is a small twist. Since there is no armhole seam, the slash and hinge must be created at the point where the armhole would have been. Place the front of your fitting pattern on top of the fashion pattern, matching the center front and the shoulder and neck points. Establish the bust point and use the fitting pattern as a guide to draw

an armhole on the fashion pattern, beginning at the point where the hinge should be and continuing up to the shoulder point. Draw the other slash lines as you normally would for this type of alteration. Beginning at the hemline, slash along these lines to the bust point, out to the hinge on the armhole, and then up to the shoulder, creating a hinge at the shoulder point. See Figure 14. Now do the alteration as you normally would.

SHOULDER ALTERATIONS ON RAGLAN AND DOLMAN SLEEVES

The shoulder alterations for both raglan and dolman styles will depend on the shape of the over-arm seam. If it is very straight, then an alteration to bring the shoulder in or out would not be necessary. If the over-arm seam does have a particular shape, altering should be done. See Figure 15. To add or subtract chest and shoulder width on a

raglan style, temporarily tape the sleeve to the bodice. Beginning at the neck point, overlap and match seamlines as far as possible, keeping the pattern flat. Draw in the L-slash, using your fitting pattern as a guide. Carefully separate the pattern pieces and correct the sleeve and bodice. Blend armhole and shoulder seamlines, as needed. See Figure 16.

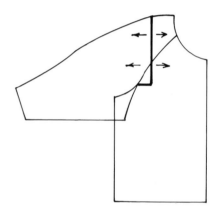

Figure 16. L-slash alteration to adjust shoulder/chest width on a raglan style.

If you only need a shoulder length correction, make a box around the shoulder point with the vertical lines 1 to $1\frac{1}{2}$ inches (2.5 to 4 cm) on either side of the shoulder point and extending down 2 inches (5 cm). Move the box in or out, adding tissue, to get the proper length. Re-curve the shoulder seam.

For the dolman style there are two possible shoulder alterations: the box method described above for the raglan sleeve or the L-slash alteration. For the L-slash alteration, draw a line from the shoulder as

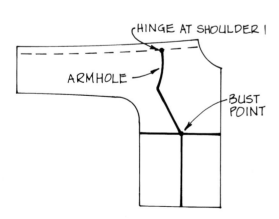

Figure 14. Slash lines for bust cup alteration on a dolman style.

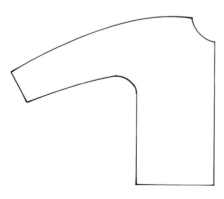

Figure 15. Shaped over-arm seam of a dolman style.

you would to make this correction on the fitting pattern, but extend the horizontal leg of the L all the way down the sleeve to the hem. See Figure 17. Slash along the lines.

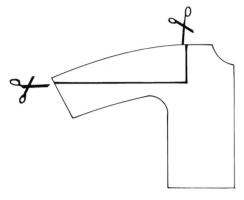

Figure 17. L-slash alteration to adjust shoulder/sleeve width on a dolman style.

Overlap the edges at the shoulder to shorten, or spread the edges apart to lengthen the sleeve. In either alteration the shoulder is corrected.

If you also need to adjust the sleeve length, the L-correction may do the trick. The lower part of the sleeve hemline was not moved. If

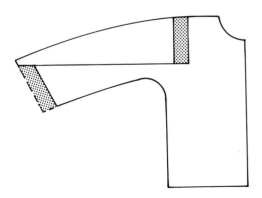

Figure 18. Adjusting dolman sleeve length after L-slash shoulder alteration.

you have lengthened the shoulder, you may need to extend the unchanged section to match the section you moved. See Figure 18. On the other hand, if you have shortened the shoulder you may have to shorten the original hemline to match the corrected portion, or you may keep the original length by adding tissue to fill in and even up.

Shoulder angles for the raglan can and should be corrected for a comfortable fit. The raglan sleeve can be one of two types: separate front and back sections or an all-in-one sleeve that usually has a shoulder dart. To alter the all-in-one shoulder-dart version to adjust for forward shoulders, draw a box around the dart and move it forward. See Figure 19. Broad shoulders require a shorter dart length,

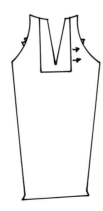

Figure 19. Adjusting one-piece sleeve for forward shoulders by moving shoulder dart with box method.

whereas sloping shoulders need a deeper dart or, even better, the addition of shoulder pads.

The shoulder seamline on the two-piece sleeve can be moved forward. Use your fitting pattern to determine the shoulder point, then redraw the seam forward of and parallel to the original, all the way to the sleeve hem. If needed, use the same technique to add to the back sleeve over-arm seamline, again making the correction all the way to the sleeve hem. See Figure 20. To correct for broad shoulders, raise the

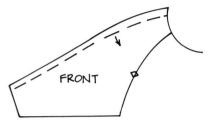

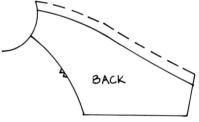

Figure 20. Adjusting two-part raglan and dolman sleeves for forward shoulders by moving front and back shoulder seamlines.

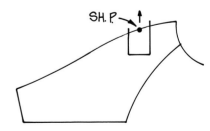

Figure 21. Adjusting raglan and dolman sleeves for broad shoulders by raising the shoulder point with the box method.

shoulder point using a box and blend to the original seam at the neck and hem. See Figure 21. Sloping shoulders can be accommodated using the box in reverse, again blending to the original seam at the neck and hem. The alterations for broad or sloping shoulders must be done on both the front and the back sections. Because there is no set-in and the armholes on the raglan and dolman styles are lower than those on the fitting pattern, it is best to alter them at the shoulders rather than raising or lowering the armhole.

Dolman shoulders can be altered in the same fashion as the two-piece raglan. If there is a dart at the shoulder, follow the procedure for the raglan sleeve. Check for other alterations by referring to your fitting pattern, including additions or subtractions to the side seams, neckline variations, and length corrections. Do a tissue fit or make a muslin to confirm all changes.

ALTERING JACKET AND COAT PATTERNS

When making jackets and coats, purchase the same size pattern you did for your dress fitting pattern and make the exact same corrections. Jackets and coats are designed with extra fitting ease since they are almost always worn over other garments. Even unstructured jackets will benefit from the bust cup correction, especially if you are a D cup

or larger, since this alteration will prevent your garment from hiking up in front and gapping at the neckline. Upper back and shoulder corrections are also necessary for good jacket and coat fitting. In addition to the alterations you always make, changes in length and width should also be made since these garments are more likely to be relatively close-fitting. As always, check the fit in both tissue and muslin before cutting your fabric.

NECKLINE GAPPING IN JACKETS

A special problem encountered in the cardigan style jacket is our old nemesis, neckline "gaposis" or gapping. This problem is usually corrected with the bust cup alteration and/or during the sewing process—by stabilizing the bias neckline edge with twill tape or other straight-of-grain material to prevent stretching. If gapping is still a problem after the bust cup correction, the following alteration can be made to the pattern tissue—it cannot be done after the fabric has been cut. On the jacket or coat with bust darts, or to create such darts, first slash from the neckline to, but not through, the bust point. Next, slash from the middle of the side dart or directly across from the bust point, as in the no-dart bodice, to, but not through, the bust point and create a hinge. Overlap the edges of the slash at the neckline, thus making it a little bit

shorter, up to $1/2$ inch (1.25 cm). See Figure 22. The correction will result in a slightly deeper bust dart. Make the same changes on lining, facings, and interfacing.

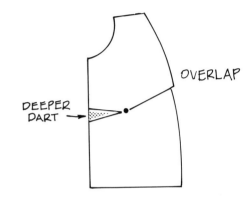

Figure 22. Correcting neckline gapping on jacket front by slashing and spreading bust dart, and slashing and overlapping front neckline edge.

THE TWO-PART SLEEVE

At first glance, it may seem difficult to transfer the corrections you have made on the conventional one-piece sleeve of the fitting pattern to the two-piece sleeve more common in fitted garments. The principle remains the same. Before any other alterations, you must make the same corrections to the sleeve at the armhole point as you have made to the bodice. The alteration procedure described below, therefore, begins with the underarm section of the two-part sleeve.

THE UNDERARM

1. On the pattern piece labeled "under sleeve," locate the circle, square, or dot that indicates the point at which the side seam of the bodice will meet the armhole seamline. This is our old friend the armhole point. Draw a line, parallel to the grainline, beginning at the under sleeve seam allowance and continuing through the armhole point down to the hemline.

2. Slash along this line to, but not through, the hemline. See Figure 23. Create a hinge at the hemline by slashing up through the hem allowance. If you also need additional width at the wrist, continue the slash through the hemline and hem allowance.

Figure 23. Slashing under sleeve from armhole point to hem, to make same amount of alteration as made to bodice.

3. To calculate the amount of alteration you are going to do here, add the **total** amount of change you made to **both** the front and back bodice pieces at the seamline. For example, if you added 2 inches (5 cm) to the front at the armhole point and 1 inch (2.5 cm) to the

back at the same point, you will have to add a total of 3 inches (7.5 cm) to the sleeve at the armhole point. Over tissue, spread apart or overlap the slash lines the needed amount. If you have made a hinge at the hemline, your correction will resemble a wedge. This correction will not violate the 1-inch (2.5-cm) rule, since the distance you have added or subtracted is the total of **both** the front and back corrections.

4. Tape the correction in place.

5. Re-establish the armhole point.

THE UPPER SLEEVE

There are three methods of altering the upper sleeve: exterior correction of the back seams of both the upper and under sleeves, for a total of up to $^{3}/_{4}$ inch (2 cm) of correction; interior slash and pivot correction used on the basic fitting pattern to add or subtract up to 1 inch (2.5 cm) at the bicep line; and the double L-slash to add even more width.

Exterior Correction to Upper and Under Sleeves

1. Draw a line perpendicular to the grainline of the under sleeve through the armhole point.

2. Matching back seamlines, continue this line across the upper sleeve, perpendicular to the grainline.

3. At the back seam of both the under sleeve and upper sleeve, measure up to $^{3}/_{8}$ inch (1 cm) beyond the original seamline and make a

mark on the lines you just drew. From this mark, blend up to zero at the armhole seam and down into the sleeve; don't let the seamline curve too much. See Figure 24.

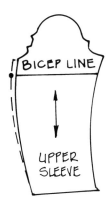

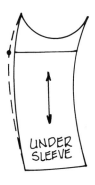

Figure 24. Exterior alteration at back seams of upper and under sleeves.

Slash and Pivot Correction to Upper Seeve

If the exterior method does not provide enough adjustment, or provides too much, perform the following slash and pivot correction. This method is an especially effective adjustment for a slender arm:

1. Draw a vertical line, parallel to the grainline, from the shoulder point (indicated by a circle or dot) to the hemline.

2. Draw a horizontal line, perpendicular to the first, from seam to seam. This line will be just above the bicep line. See Figure 25.

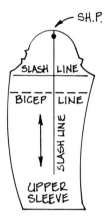

Figure 25. Altering upper sleeve with slash and pivot method.

3. Clip the seam allowances at the top, hem, and two sides in preparation for creating hinges.

4. Beginning at the center, slash along both lines to, but not through, the seams and hemline to create the hinges.

5. Place pattern on top of tissue, spread apart up to a total of 1 inch (2.5 cm), and tape in place. Do the reverse for a slender arm.

6. To complete the correction, measure and reestablish the cap line, as described on page 66, to provide the needed 1 to 2 inches (2.5 to 5 cm) of ease.

Double L-Slash Correction to Upper Sleeve

If the exterior or interior methods do not provide enough adjustment, perform the following double L-slash correction:

1. Locate and draw the horizontal bicep line on the upper sleeve pattern piece.

2. Draw two vertical lines from the bicep line up through the sleeve cap seam allowance, on either side of the shoulder point. See Figure 26.

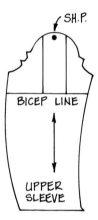

Figure 26. Altering upper sleeve with double L-slash alteration.

3. Cut out the two mirror image L-sections you have created and slide each one out the needed amounts along the bicep line until you have achieved the necessary correction.

4. Double-check the relationship between the total length of the armhole seamline on the bodice and the seamline around the entire sleeve, including the underarm and sleeve cap. In a jacket, there should be a total of 1 to 2 inches (2.5 to 5 cm) of

ease in the sleeve cap to be absorbed into the bodice armhole. Adjust the height of the sleeve cap and, if necessary, reposition the shoulder point to achieve this balance.

MOCK TWO-PART SLEEVE

This sleeve style combines the benefits of the two-part sleeve with the ease of one-part sleeve construction. It is designed to be cut in one piece. See Figure 27. Altering this sleeve style is similar to changing the conventional one-part sleeve of the fitting pattern:

Figure 27. Mock two-part sleeve.

1. Draw a line from the armhole point, parallel to the grainline, down through the hemline and hem allowance. On this sleeve style, the armhole point is usually indicated by a circle or square at the lowest point in the dip of the armhole seamline.

2. Draw in the bicep line perpendicular to the grainline and intersecting the armhole points.

3. Cut along the line from armhole point to hem, separating the sleeve into two pieces. See Figure 28.

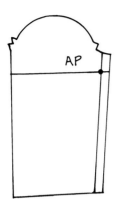

Figure 28. Slash line from armhole point to hem, for altering mock two-part sleeve.

4. Transfer the smaller of the two pieces to the back of the sleeve, overlapping seamlines from armhole to hem. See Figure 29.

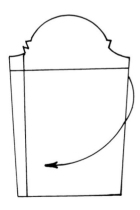

Figure 29. Moving slashed segment of mock two-part sleeve. Once sleeve alteration is complete, slashed segment is returned to its original position.

5. Tape temporarily in place and alter just like you did the sleeve of your fitting pattern.

6. Once the alteration is complete, un-tape the two parts and return the smaller piece to its original position.

7. Blend and true all seamlines, as needed.

ALTERING CENTER FRONT BUTTON CLOSURES

Once you have corrected the bust cup, make an individualized buttonhole guide to solve the problem of any gapping at the center front. The key areas of concern here are the neckline, the fullest part of the bust, and the waistline. The top button should start one button-width below the finished neckline and there should be a button at the point where your bustline crosses the center front. There should also be a button at the waistline, but if this cannot be accomplished while maintaining even spacing between buttons once the neckline and bustline button placements have been deter-

mined, put a snap or hook and eye at the waistline. See Figure 30.

Once you have established these two or three points, simply distribute any other buttons evenly along the length of the closure. Ideally, buttons should be $2^{1}/_{2}$ to $3^{1}/_{2}$ inches (6.5 to 9 cm) apart. The buttonholes should begin $^{1}/_{8}$ inch (3 mm) beyond the center line on the front extension and should be equal in length to the button width plus its thickness. Stabilize all buttonhole plackets and extensions with interfacing as well as a facing. Always sew and test a trial buttonhole before putting buttonholes in your garment.

SHOULDER PADS

An important consideration in evaluating a fashion pattern's fit is whether or not it calls for shoulder pads. This is especially important for jackets and coats. If the pattern does not call for pads and you usually wear them, you can add them by raising the shoulder point both in

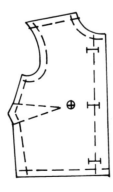

Figure 30. Correct buttonhole spacing with buttonholes just below neckline, at bust level, and at waistline.

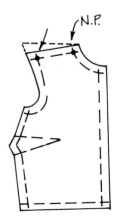

Figure 31. Raising shoulder point for addition of shoulder pads.

the front and back an amount equal to the thickness of the pads, and then redrawing the shoulder lines, blending to the original neck point. See Figure 31. Conversely, if you do not like shoulder pads and the pattern calls for them, you will have to subtract the thickness of the pads by lowering the shoulder point, since room has been provided for them by the pattern-maker.

ALTERING SKIRTS

Alterations to skirts generally follow the basic fitting pattern. The major corrections to the prominent curves should be done first. A six- or seven-gore skirt may present special problems. The corrections are made in basically the same manner as on your fitting pattern:

1. For a prominent curve, draw a horizontal line from the center front abdomen and/or back seat, as needed, at approximately the same location as you did on the fitting pattern.

2. On the side panel, draw a horizontal line at the same level as the center panel from the side front or side back seam to the middle of the panel.

3. Draw a diagonal line from this point up to the side waist point.

4. Then, from the point in the middle of the side panel where your horizontal line ended, draw a line straight up to the waistline. See Figure 32.

5. On the center panel, slash and spread from the center along the

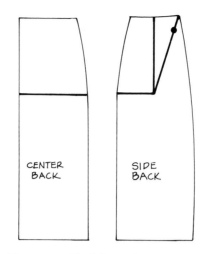

Figure 32. Slash lines for prominent seat curve alteration on gored skirt.

horizontal line the amount needed, as on your fitting pattern.

6. Cut the side panel across to the middle and then diagonally up to the waist point, creating a hinge there by clipping the seam allowance.

7. Then slash down the vertical line from the waist, creating another

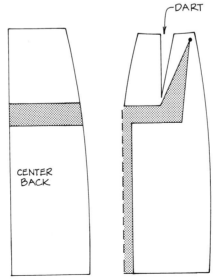

Figure 33. Adding width and length to seat curve of gored skirt.

hinge just above the horizontal slash. See Figure 33.

8. Using the center panel as a guide, spread the edges apart. The horizontal opening in the side should be the same as in the center panel. V-shaped wedges will open along the diagonal and vertical slashes.

9. Fill with tissue, pin and tape in place, and blend seamlines and cutting lines.

This correction adds circumference to the waist. If you do not need this, it can be absorbed by creating a waist dart or, if the skirt is

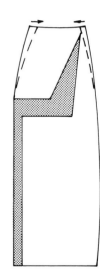

Figure 34. Reducing unneeded width at waist after making prominent curve alteration.

gathered or has pleats, by distributing the extra width in these. If you prefer, it can also be eliminated at the seams. See Figure 34. This completes the prominent curve alteration. You must, however, check the total hip circumference because this alteration alone may not give you enough width. Double-check this area during the tissue fit. If you need still more width, add equally to the side back and side front seams. Re-curve the seam, blending up to the waistline. When blending down to the hem, do not taper; instead, keep the addition even. See Figure 35.

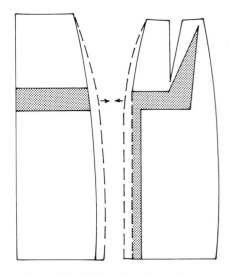

Figure 35. Adding hip circumference at side seams after making prominent curve alteration.

If you have a skirt with a gathered waist, this major correction can be performed in either the front or the back, as needed. Make the same slashes on your fashion pattern as you made on the fitting pattern, adding slash lines where the darts would be. Spread apart, to increase width and length. This alteration adds width at the waistline; if it is not needed, it can be easily absorbed into the gathers. These changes will ensure that the hem

falls evenly around the entire circumference of the skirt.

A flared skirt is relatively fitted through the hips. Making the abdominal or seat alteration you did on your fitting pattern will result in a smoother fit and a more even hemline. The flared skirt may not have darts, so use the instructions above for a gathered skirt as your guide. If there are pre-existing darts, use your fitting pattern as a guide. Any other length and width corrections you made on your fitting pattern should also be made to the fashion pattern. In very full, extremely flared skirts the hip circumference may not need to be corrected unless you want to maintain the exact amount of design ease intended by the designer.

Pocket gapping can sometimes be a problem in both skirts and pants. But you will find that once you have solved the prominent curve and additional circumference problems and made any needed changes to the hip curve, the pockets will cease gapping, unless they gap because of a sewing problem.

ALTERING PANTS

Pants alterations will depend on the style. For example, a full-leg trouser or palazzo pant requires a longer crotch length and sometimes a longer crotch depth than provided in your fitting pattern. To preserve this design feature, you must make the same crotch corrections as you

did in your fitting pattern. Compare your fitting pattern to the front and back crotch seam of the fashion pattern. Do you need more length? Should the crotch curve be redrawn? Check to see whether the crotch points are comparable; in fuller styles, crotch extensions should be longer to allow for the greater width in the thigh. If you made a prominent curve or wedge correction to your fitting pattern, you should make the same changes to the fashion pattern, referring to the information on the skirt corrections above and to your pants fitting pattern. All other width and length corrections to your fitting pattern should also be made here.

NOTE: Some apparent fitting problems are really sewing problems. Therefore, sew test seams on all fabrics that you think might be troublesome, experimenting with different stitches, stitch lengths, needles, and threads until you have achieved a smooth, pucker-free stitching line. Take special care not to stretch bias seams. Stitch accurate seam allowances—especially on princess line garments, which may have as many as eight vertical seams. Even slight inaccuracies will result in considerable fitting distortion.

You will discover that the only drawback to your new proficiency at achieving good fit is that you are now much more demanding! But it's a great reason to create a brand new wardrobe that fits perfectly.

Chapter Ten

Using your personal fitting patterns as design tools

"Isn't this fun? The dart has moved all around the bodice and has come back home!"

—*Sally, to an amazed student*

The design suggestions we make in this chapter are fairly simple, but the possibilities are endless. The most important thing to keep in mind as you experiment with your own variations is that hidden inside every garment is a "skeleton"—the basic fitted dress or fitted pants you have already mastered. By using your own fitting pattern as a design tool, you will eliminate virtually **all** fitting problems in the garments you create. This chapter will show you how to manipulate curves and darts, and how to vary the internal width (and, therefore, the design ease) of virtually every area in a dress or pants—bodice, sleeves, skirt, and pant legs.

When you set out to create a new style from your fitting pattern, you must first copy or fuse your adjusted pattern onto poster board or oak tag. Either one will be better for pattern-making than tissue or interfacing. If you choose to copy your pattern, you need not mark the details of all the additions and deletions you have made, but you do need to transfer all seamlines, darts, and other pattern markings such as notches, dots or circles, and grainlines. If you are going to eliminate the center front or center back seam by laying your pattern along a fold, omit the seam allowance along that side on your new pattern and mark it with the traditional symbol for a fold. When doing any pattern-making, always trace a copy of your poster board fitting pattern to another, lighter-weight paper; then, create your pattern designs from the copy, which is easier to manipulate and keeps your original pattern safe for the next time.

Variations in the design ease of the bodice, skirt, sleeve, and pants are accomplished by simple methods: moving the darts from their conventional position, making even or uneven interior changes for the length and width of the garment or section, or a combination of these methods.

Basic Fitting Terms

Almost no new terms or techniques remain for you to learn—you are now a graduate student! You have command of all the basic fitting terminology and alteration skills, and you're ready to be your own designer. All that is left is one easy design term and a brief review of the types of paper you might use for this final exercise.

TORSO DRESS. A semi-fitted dress with no waist seam, a relaxed fit at the waist, and a straight line to the hem.

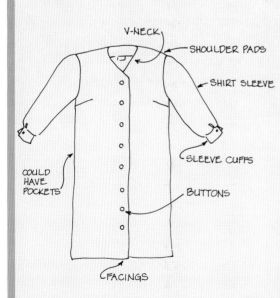

Pattern-making papers

Pattern tissue paper is too fragile to stand up to the demands of pattern-making and the repeated use of a pattern once it is perfected. Non-woven interfacing is also inappropriate for patterns that will be stored for a long time and constantly re-used. Therefore, you will want to consider the various pattern-making papers available. The following are all good and durable options:

ALPHABET PAPER. Sold in better fabric stores, this paper comes on rolls, is 45 inches (1.1 m) wide, and is pre-marked with a grid to aid in transferring measurements and markings. It is the approximate weight of bond typing paper.

BROWN PAPER BAG. Easily available at the supermarket—and the price is right! Cut open and spread out, conventional paper bags are sturdy and a good size for most pattern pieces—especially the larger ones.

NEWSPRINT. Used for ordinary newspapers, this can be purchased in large sheets from art suppliers or as end roles from newspaper printers.

OAK TAG or MANILA. Similar in weight and color to manila file folders and poster board. This is the ideal substance on which to fuse your fitting pattern and then use to create your own designs. It is sturdy, provides a good edge for tracing, and will hold up to repeated usage. Expensive if bought in long rolls from paper and art supply houses; large-sized poster board can often be substituted.

VELLUM. So named because it resembles the very fine goat skin on which medieval parchments were written, many of which are still in existence nearly one thousand years later! Vellum resembles a sturdy onion skin and is semi-transparent, making tracing relatively easy. It is often sold on rolls in finer fabric stores and art supply houses. Its one drawback is that it can become brittle with age and repeated use.

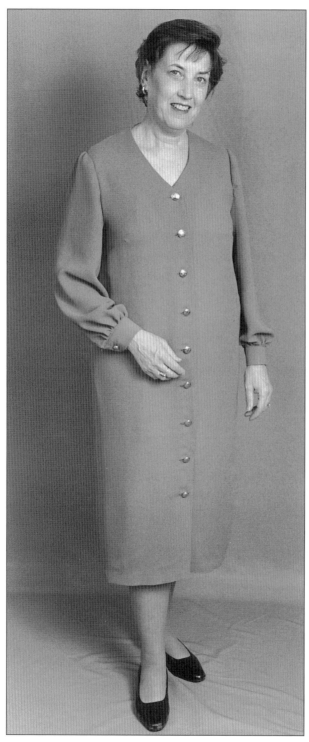

The personalized fitting pattern can be used as a design tool for creating new garments. Here, the basic pattern is transformed into a loosely-fitted V-neck torso dress with button front and shirt-style sleeves.

USING YOUR BASIC PATTERN TO DESIGN A NEW DRESS

To illustrate how these changes operate, we will begin by giving your personal dress pattern a brand new silhouette and adding some distinctive design details. As it exists now, the basic pattern is for a fitted dress with a jewel neck, fitted sleeves, bust and waist darts in the bodice, waist darts in the narrow skirt, and a back closure ending at the hipline. You will transform it into a more loosely fitted straight torso dress with a V-neck, buttons down the front, and shirt-style cuffed sleeves.

Begin the transformation with the bodice front. Trace a copy of this piece of your fitting pattern onto pattern paper; be sure to include the bust point. You will move the bust dart in the front to the waist and eventually open the waist dart out to achieve the new straighter side seamline. Follow these steps:

1. Begin by extending the ends of the darts to the bust point.

2. Slash along the lower leg of the bust dart from the side seam to, but not through, the bust point.

3. Slash along the outside leg of the waist dart up to, but not through, the bust point, leaving a hinge between your two slashes at the bust point.

4. Rotate the lower outside portion of the bodice out until you have closed the bust dart, bringing the dart legs together at the side seam. Temporarily tape the bust dart closed. See Figure 1. The waist dart has become wider and will be used in the next step. You have just completed the pattern-making process called "dart manipulation," which means, very simply, moving a dart from one place to another.

5. The next step will be to move some of the waist dart to the shoulder, while at the same time making the side seam parallel to the center front. From the midpoint of the shoulder seam, draw a line to the bust point.

6. Slash along the line to, but not through, the bust point and leave a hinge.

7. Place enough paper under the entire bodice and below the waistline to complete the dress pattern all the way to the bottom hem.

8. Working on the cork or foam core mat, place the bodice at the top of the paper and pin the center front area. The side front is movable because of the bust point hinge.

9. Move the side into the desired position, making the side seamline parallel to the center front. The waist dart may get a little smaller, and a shoulder dart will be created. See Figure 2. Here, again, is dart manipulation.

10. Tape the entire pattern down except for the armhole area and shoulder dart, as these will be moved again later.

To create the lower half of the dress, follow these steps:

1. Extend the center front and side seamlines to the bottom of the paper; they should be parallel to each other.

2. Match the skirt center front waist from the original pattern to the new bodice center front waist, and make guide marks on the new paper at the

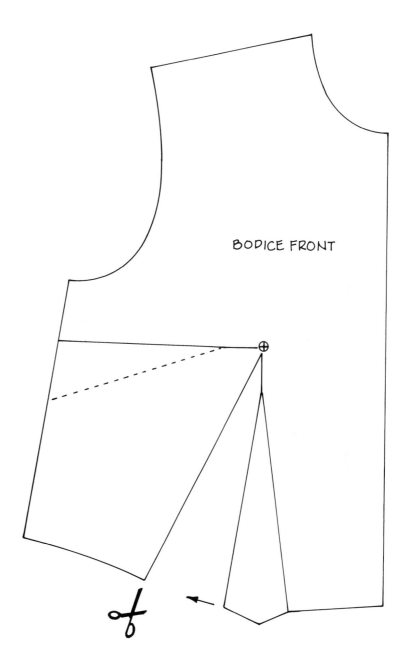

Figure 1. To begin transforming the fitting pattern into the torso dress, the bust dart is closed by rotating the side front of the bodice outward.

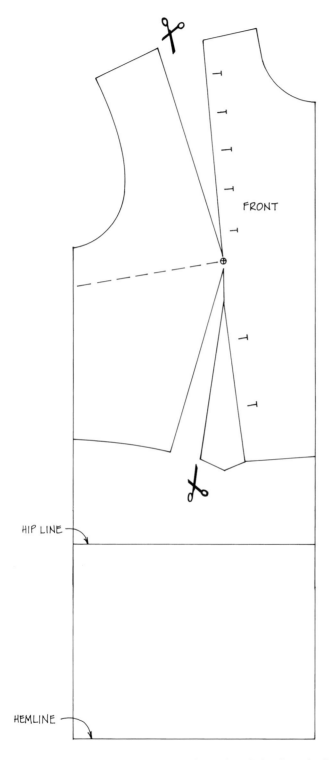

HIP LINE

HEMLINE

Figure 2. The side seam is straightened and the front bodice is lengthened to a dress length.

points where the hipline and hemline intersect the center line.

3. Next, match the original skirt side seam waist point to the new bodice waist point, and again make guide marks where the hipline and hemline cross the side seamline. See Figure 2.

4. With the hip curve or Fashion Ruler, connect the marks to form the new hipline and hemline.

Now turn your attention to the back and trace the original back bodice onto pattern paper. The next procedure is similar to the one you employed in front, but you don't have to move any darts. Follow these steps:

1. Draw a diagonal line from the point of the waist dart to the armhole notch or dot.

2. Slash along the outer leg of the waist dart from the waist to the dart point and, from there, diagonally to, but not through, the armhole seamline.

3. Clip the seam allowance to create a hinge at the armhole seam.

4. As you did on the front, place paper under the bodice and secure the center back area. The lower side back remains movable.

5. Spread open the side so that the side seam is parallel to the center back.

6. Extend the center back and side seamlines down to the bottom of the paper, keeping the lines parallel.

7. Determine and mark the hipline and hemline in the same manner as you did in the front. See Figure 3.

You now have essentially created a torso dress pattern. A few measurements still need to be checked and some additional ease must be added. Measure and compare the hip circumference of the new pattern with the fitting pattern. What differences do you find? If you need to add more to the hipline of the new dress, add half the addition to the front, the other half to the back, and continue the addition down to the hemline. Blend up from the addition at the hipline to the waistline. Check the side seams to see if the front and back guide marks line up. With a ruler, begin at the front armhole and check the length to the waist point; then check the distance between the waist and the hipline, and the hipline to the hemline. Compare the front to the back at the side seam. All points should line up and the pattern should lie flat. All guide marks must match at the armhole point, side waist point, hipline, and hemline.

ADDING EASE

To accommodate the additional fitting ease required by the relaxed style of the new dress, lower the armhole point 1/4 inch (6 mm) on both the front and back patterns and extend it out 1/2 inch (1.25 cm). Redraw the armhole, as needed, and extend the side seam out 1/2 inch (1.25 cm) along the entire length of both the front and back pattern pieces. See Figure 3.

MOVING THE SHOULDER DART

The front shoulder dart should now be displaced to the side seam, as follows:

1. Loosen the tape from the side dart and rotate the shoulder dart until it is closed.

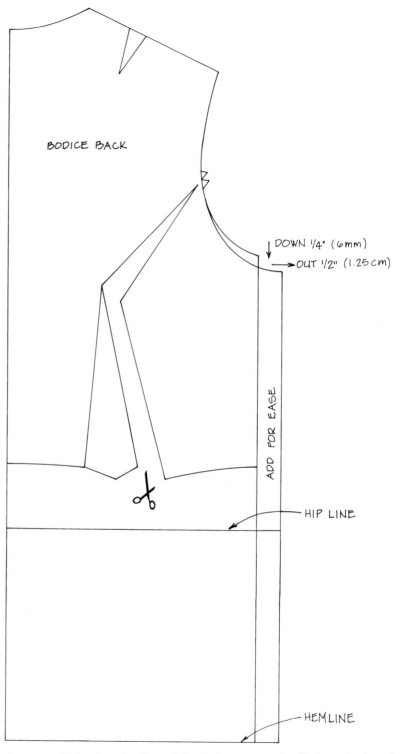

Figure 3. The back waist dart of the fitting pattern is eliminated when the side seam is straightened and back bodice is lengthened for the torso dress. To achieve the looser style of the torso dress at the armhole, extra fitting ease is added to the fitting pattern.

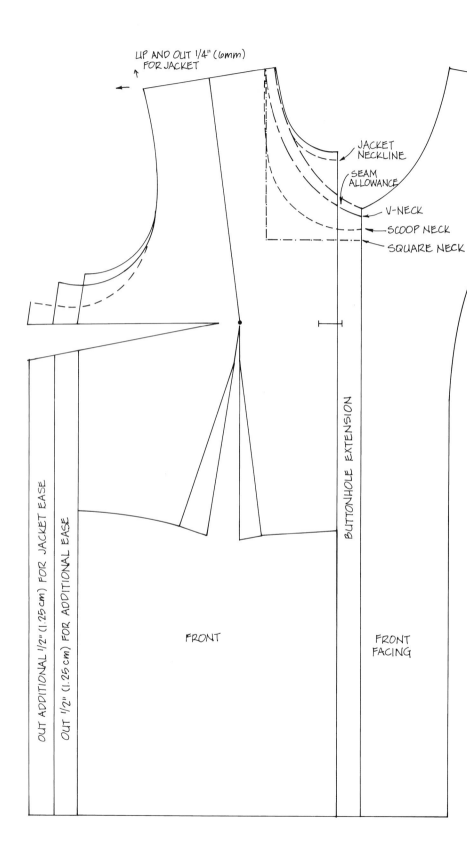

UP AND OUT 1/4" (6mm)
FOR JACKET

JACKET
NECKLINE

SEAM
ALLOWANCE

V-NECK

SCOOP NECK

SQUARE NECK

BUTTONHOLE EXTENSION

OUT ADDITIONAL 1/2" (1.25cm) FOR JACKET EASE

OUT 1/2" (1.25 cm) FOR ADDITIONAL EASE

FRONT

FRONT
FACING

Figure 4. After closing the bust dart of the fitting pattern and straightening the side seam, the shoulder dart is then closed; this re-opens a smaller-than-original bust dart, which helps shape the dress front for a better fit. The jewel neckline of the fitting pattern can be varied in a number of ways: V-neck, scoop, or square. A buttonhole extension is added to the center front of the fitting pattern, for the button front closure of the torso dress. Front and back neckline facings are then added. For a jacket, the armhole point is lowered and more ease is added at the side seam, extra ease is added at the shoulder point for shoulder pads, and the front neckline is lowered.

2. Secure both the shoulder and side dart with tape. The bust dart has now traveled around the pattern and come back home! It is a smaller dart than it was originally because some of it has been displaced to the waist. Sewing the bust dart will give a better hang to the finished garment, especially if you have larger than a B cup.

3. Redraw the bust dart using the upper leg as your guide; the dart point should be 1 to $1^{1}/_{2}$ inches (2.5 to 4 cm) from the bust point. See Figure 4.

4. Fold the dart to the closed position to re-establish the side seam and the base of the dart.

5. Add the seam allowance, if need be, and cut away the extra paper.

6. Transfer this version onto poster board or oak tag to serve as the master pattern for a torso dress.

DESIGNING A NEW NECKLINE

Changing the shape of your fitting pattern's neckline is relatively easy. Mark the point where you want the neckline to be at the center front. Next, mark the point where you want the neckline to intersect with the shoulder seamline. Connect the two points with a slightly curved line for a V-neck, a more curved line for a scoop neck, or two lines at right angles to one another for a square neck. Then, add a seam allowance. See Figure 4. A tissue fit is a good idea at this point to be certain there is no gapping at the neckline. If there is, review page 106 to see how to cure it.

Button and Buttonhole Placement

Once the neckline is done, the buttonholes and buttons are the next consideration. To add the buttonhole extension, first measure the width of the buttons you are going to use. You may need to tape more paper along the front edge of the pattern from the shoulder level to the hem; a strip 6 inches (15 cm) wide should be enough. Make the buttonhole extension by drawing a line parallel to the center front from neckline to hem. The extension should be the width of your button. See Figure 4. This line will eventually become either the fold line for a self-facing or the seamline at which you will attach a separate facing.

To determine correct buttonhole spacing, review page 109. Traditionally, buttonholes are placed horizontally in dressy garments and vertically in sporty styles. The closure on women's garments is right side over left in the front, and left over right in the back. On men's garments and unisex styles, the front closes left over right.

Adding Front and Neckline Facing

You now must create the facings required by the new torso dress. The strip of paper you added to the front edge of the buttonhole extension will also serve as the facing pattern for this part of the dress. Follow these steps:

1. Fold the paper to the underside along the fold line or seamline of the buttonhole extension, not along the center front line.

2. Trim the paper even with the shoulder line, the new neckline, and hemline.

3. Unfold it and you will see the beginnings of the front facing.

4. The finished facing should be between 2 and $2^1/2$ inches (5 and 6.5 cm) wide along its entire length. Measure from the neck point down the shoulder of the facing and make a mark $2^1/4$ to $2^3/4$ inches (5.5 to 7 cm) from the neck point. You will have an extra $^1/4$ inch (6 mm) that can be turned under to finish the outside edge of the facing.

5. At the hemline, measure and mark the same amount out from the fold line or seamline of the buttonhole extension.

6. Draw a line parallel to the fold line from the hem up to the level of the bust point.

7. From the shoulder mark you made, draw a gently curved line that connects at the bustline with the line you just drew up from the hem. See Figure 4.

8. Trim away the extra paper along the outside edge of the facing. You have now created a self-facing along the front extension edge. If you cut along the extension line and add seam allowances to both the extension and the facing, you can sew a separate facing.

To make the back neckline facing, follow these steps:

1. Place the back pattern piece over a new piece of pattern paper that is at least 3 inches (7.5 cm) wider than the back neck opening and extends down at least 3 inches (7.5 cm) below the lowest point on the neck opening.

2. Trace along the center back cutting or fold line, beginning $2^3/4$ inches (7 cm) below the neckline. Then trace the neck and along the shoulder seam, ending $2^3/4$

inches (7 cm) down from the neck point. Again, the extra $^1/4$ inch (6 mm) is for finishing the outside edge of the facing.

3. Draw the outside edge of the facing, curving from the point you made on the shoulder seam to the point at the center back. See Figure 5.

4. Transfer any notches or other pattern markings.

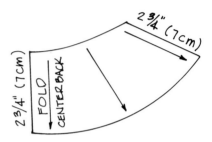

Figure 5. The back pattern piece is used to trace a back neckline facing for the torso dress.

FINISHING TOUCHES

You must consider whether or not you want shoulder pads in this dress. If you do, raise the shoulder point on both the front and the back the thickness of the shoulder pad; draw a seamline from the new shoulder point to the original neck point. See Figure 6. To add pockets at the side seam, see the section on pockets in trousers or slacks later in this chapter.

VARIATIONS ON THE TORSO DRESS

The straight torso dress pattern you have now completed can serve a number of purposes. If you cut it off at the hipline, it becomes a blouse. If you leave it sleeveless and lower the armhole an

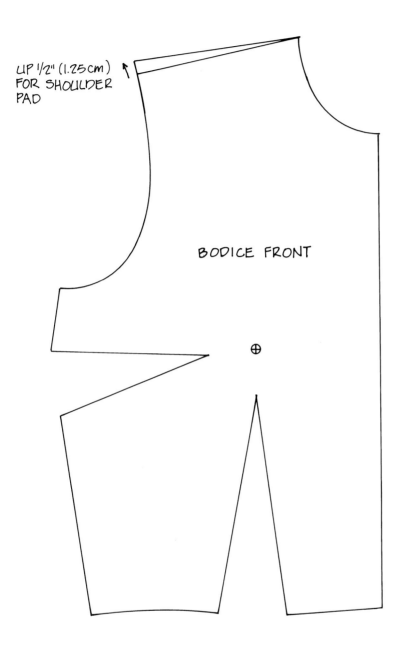

UP 1/2" (1.25cm)
FOR SHOULDER
PAD

BODICE FRONT

Figure 6. To make room for shoulder pads, the shoulder point is raised the thickness of the pads and the seamline is tapered to the original neck point.

additional $1/2$ inch (1.25 cm), over and above the $1/4$ inch (6 mm) adjustment you already made to convert the fitting pattern to an unfitted blouse or dress, it can become a vest or tunic. To develop a jacket pattern, you simply add $1/2$ inch (1.25 cm) to the side seams and lower the armhole point another $1/2$ inch (1.25 cm) beyond the changes you have already made. You will also need to extend the shoulder seam out and up $1/4$ inch (6 mm) at the shoulder point and lower it $1/8$ inch (3 mm) at the neckline to allow for the fact that jackets are worn over other garments. See Figure 4.

Additional flare can be added to a dress, blouse, vest, tunic, or jacket by making two or more vertical slashes from the front and back hems up to hinges on the armhole, shoulder, and/or neckline seams and spreading the bottom edges apart. See Figure 7. This is called an "uneven interior change," as opposed to the even interior change you used to add or subtract width in the skirt pattern of the fitting pattern.

SLEEVE VARIATIONS

In addition to varying the torso of the dress, you can make a number of changes to the sleeves. To vary the sleeves, you must first make the same changes at the armhole point that you made to the front and back dress pieces: for a dress, $1/4$ inch (6 mm) down and

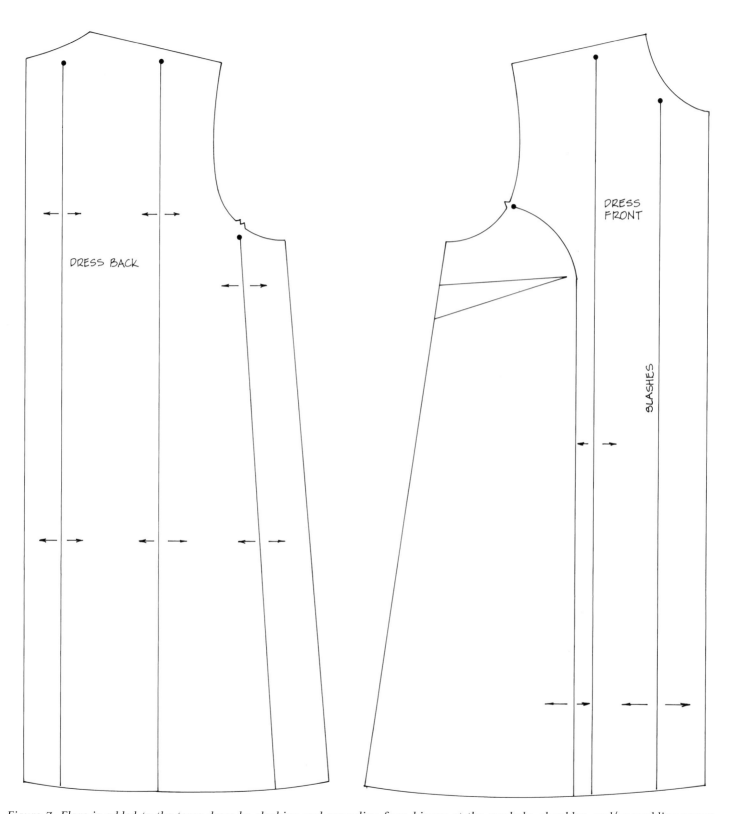

DRESS BACK

DRESS FRONT

SLASHES

Figure 7. Flare is added to the torso dress by slashing and spreading from hinges at the armhole, shoulder, and/or neckline seams.

¹/₂ inch (1.25 cm) out, blending to the original hem; for a jacket, an additional ¹/₂ inch (1.25 cm) out and ¹/₂ inch (1.25 cm) down, and ¹/₄ inch (6 mm) out at the hem on each side, blending to the underarm seam. See Figure 8. Transfer all sleeve variations to poster board or oak tag so you can use them again. On a jacket sleeve, you must also provide for the addition you have already made at the bodice shoulder by providing a bit of extra length to the sleeve cap. To do this, cut horizontally across the sleeve cap in the area above the notches and spread open ¹/₄ inch (6 mm) evenly along the entire slash. If you will be adding shoulder pads, spread the opening the ¹/₄ inch (6 mm) plus the thickness of the shoulder pads. See Figure 8.

Straight Sleeve

One of the simplest sleeve variations is to create a dartless straight sleeve. Follow these steps:

1. Trace the fitting pattern sleeve onto new pattern paper.

2. Extend the two underarm seams from the armhole point at either end of the bicep line to the hemline, keeping them parallel to one another and to the grainline. See Figure 9. Since the hemline is perpendicular to the grainline, use the front hem of the original sleeve as a guide for the length.

3. To give the sleeve more flare, make two or more uneven interior

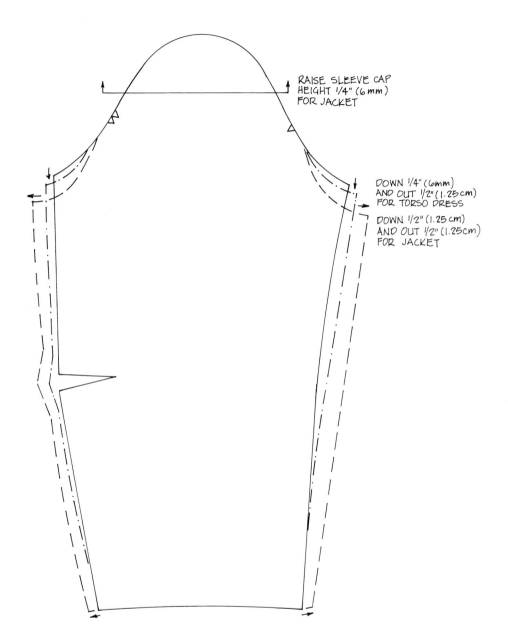

RAISE SLEEVE CAP HEIGHT ¹/₄" (6 mm) FOR JACKET

DOWN ¹/₄" (6mm) AND OUT ¹/₂" (1.25 cm) FOR TORSO DRESS

DOWN ¹/₂" (1.25 cm) AND OUT ¹/₂" (1.25cm) FOR JACKET

Figure 8. To begin varying the sleeve fitting pattern, ease is added at the armhole. For a jacket, the sleeve cap height is also altered.

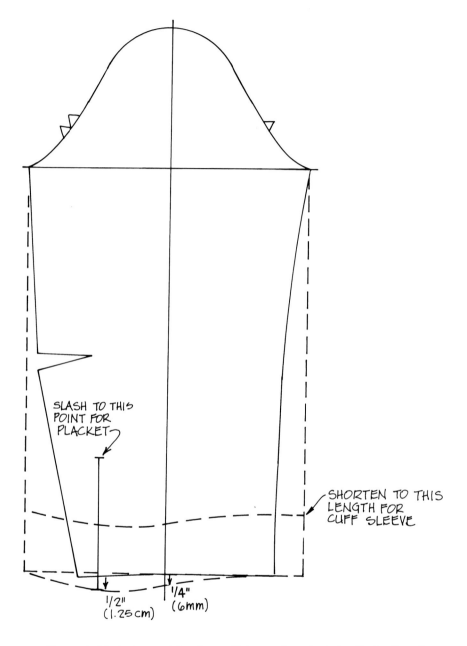

SLASH TO THIS
POINT FOR
PLACKET

SHORTEN TO THIS
LENGTH FOR
CUFF SLEEVE

1/2"
(1.25 cm)

1/4"
(6mm)

Figure 9. Variations to the sleeve fitting pattern include eliminating the elbow dart and straightening the side seams, and creating a cuffed shirt sleeve with placket.

changes by the method described for the torso. (This sleeve, with its straight hem, should be used if there are to be no cuffs. See Figure 11A.)

Shirt Sleeve

To turn the sleeve into a traditional cuffed shirt sleeve, follow these steps:

1. Trace the straight sleeve you just created onto new pattern paper.

2. Locate and mark the center of the dartless sleeve at the bottom edge.

3. Locate and mark the center of the back half at the bottom edge.

4. From the first mark, measure and mark a point 1/4 inch (6 mm) below the edge.

5. From the second mark, measure and mark a point 1/2 inch (1.25 cm) below the edge.

6. Draw a curved line from the back underarm seamline down to the 1/2-inch (1.25-cm) mark and up to the 1/4-inch (6-mm) mark. Continue the curve until you blend in to the original sleeve bottom at the front underarm seamline. See Figure 9. This sleeve with a curved hem should only be used if there are to be cuffs.

The mid-back point, where the sleeve bottom is longest, is where you will make the placket. Follow these steps:

1. Draw a line about 3 inches (7.5 cm) long and parallel to the grainline. See Figure 9. You will slash along this line when sewing the placket.

2. For the facing-like strip required to finish the slash, make a rectangle 1 1/2 inches (4 cm) wide by twice as long as the slash, including the hem seam allowance. The strip has a 1/4-inch (6-mm) seam allowance on the long edges and, when sewn, it will have a finished width of $^1/_2$ inch (1.25 cm). Refer to your favorite sewing book for specific instructions about how to sew a continuous sleeve placket.

Sleeve Cuff

The cuff itself is relatively simple—a rectangle 2 inches (5 cm) wide and cut on the straight of grain. Follow these steps:

1. To determine the correct circumference for your cuff, hold your fingers out straight and as close together as possible. Measure the distance around your hand at the knuckles.

2. Subtract $^1/_2$ inch (1.25 cm) and add the extensions you will need for the buttons and buttonholes. The finished extension should equal the width of the buttons you will be using.

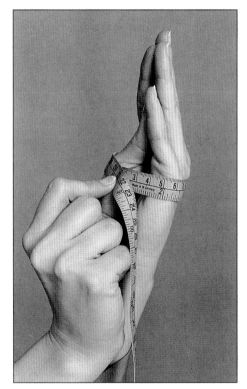

Measuring hand circumference to determine cuff size.

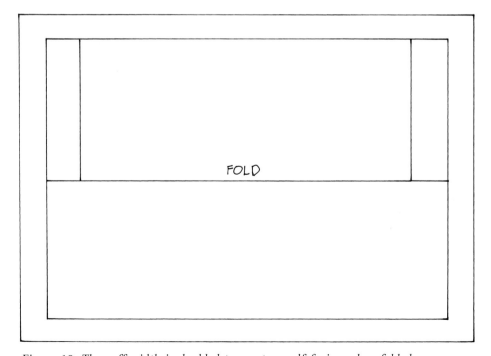

FOLD

Figure 10. The cuff width is doubled to create a self-facing when folded.

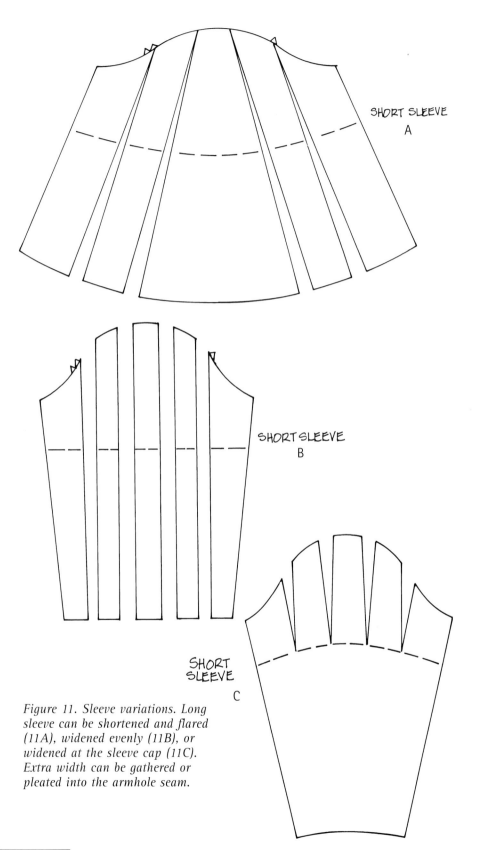

Figure 11. Sleeve variations. Long sleeve can be shortened and flared (11A), widened evenly (11B), or widened at the sleeve cap (11C). Extra width can be gathered or pleated into the armhole seam.

3. Draw a rectangle 2 inches (5 cm) wide by a length that equals your hand measurement plus twice the width of your buttons, minus $1/2$ inch (1.25 cm).

4. Double the 2-inch (5-cm) width you need for the finished cuff and add seam allowances—your cuff now has a self-facing. See Figure 10.

5. Finally, shorten the sleeve 2 inches (5 cm), since you don't want the addition of the cuff to make the sleeve too long. To help you do this accurately, you can draw lengthen/shorten lines, using your fitting pattern as a guide; this will preserve the curved lower edge.

6. Fullness can be added to the sleeve by making two or more even or uneven interior changes, as described earlier. The sleeve will then be gathered into the cuff.

Short Sleeve

If you wish short sleeves, begin by making the underarm seam change required for a dartless straight sleeve and determine the desired length. Short sleeves can end at a finished length of 2 inches (5 cm) below the armhole point, anywhere above the elbow, or just below the elbow. Be sure to allow for a hem at the bottom edge. Short sleeves can also be given added fullness by even or uneven interior changes. This fullness can be turned into a flare, if uneven changes are made along the hemline. See Figure 11A. Gathering or pleats along the armhole can be created by making even changes (see Figure 11B) or by making uneven changes that open out along the sleeve cap (see Figure 11C).

DESIGNING A SKIRT

If you wish to make a skirt from your basic dress pattern, you've got many options. Trace the skirt pieces of the fitting pattern onto new pattern paper. An easy variation is to turn the waist darts into pleats or gathers. If you want the skirt to retain a relatively straight line but wish a bit more design ease, you can add this by making the even interior change you have already utilized on the sleeve. See Figure 12.

Flare can be added by closing the darts and moving them to the hem. This is accomplished by drawing a line through the center of each dart and down to the hem. Slash along the line through the center of each dart to the dart point; then, along the same line, slash up from the hem to the dart point, leaving a hinge. Rotate the pieces until the waist darts close and wedges open below them. See Figure 13. Note that, when the darts are closed, not as much flare is added to the back hemline as to the front. The flare, therefore, will have to be equalized. Determine the total circumference measurement of the front and back hem. Divide that measurement in half and adjust both the front and the back to evenly distribute the total measurement between them.

If you wish additional flare, place the skirt pattern on a large piece of pattern paper, then slash and spread the pattern from hem to waist. You can add up to 2 inches (5 cm) of flare to both the front and back side seams at the hem, blending up to the hipline.

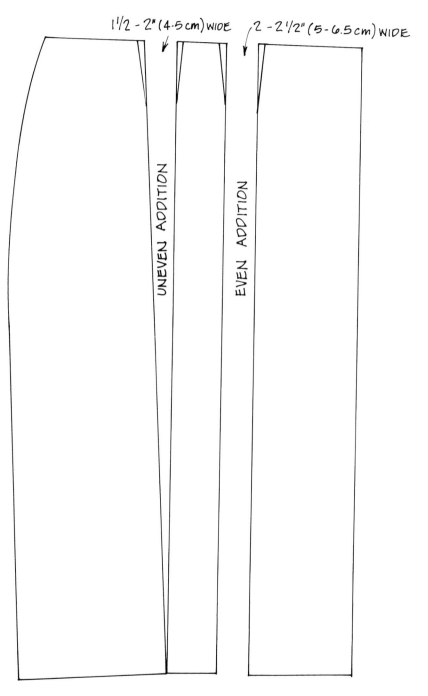

1½ - 2" (4.5 cm) WIDE   2 - 2½" (5 - 6.5 cm) WIDE

UNEVEN ADDITION

EVEN ADDITION

Figure 12. The skirt fitting pattern can be varied by eliminating waist darts and adding ease evenly or unevenly. Extra ease can be pleated or gathered at the waist.

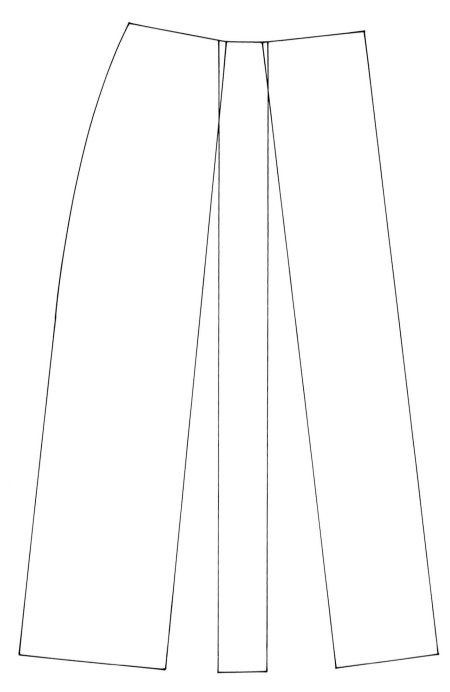

Figure 13. Adding flare to the skirt fitting pattern.

PLEATS

If you wish fullness at the waist to be absorbed into either pleats or gathers, you can make additional even or uneven internal changes. To make darts wider for trouser pleats in your skirt front, slash down the middle of the darts to the hem. If you leave a hinge at the hem edge and spread the dart, you have made an uneven internal change to create more fullness at the waist. If you spread evenly along the slash from waist to hemline, you have made an even internal change to add equal fullness. See Figure 12.

You can make both darts wider. A good first pleat width is 2 to $2\frac{1}{2}$ inches (5 to 6.5 cm) wide before sewing; the second pleat could be $1\frac{1}{2}$ to 2 inches (4 to 5 cm) wide. The outside dart can be spread either evenly or unevenly, but the center darts are usually opened evenly. If there is no second dart, you can create one by drawing, cutting, and spreading a slash line from the waist to the hem.

To finish pleats, mark the fold lines and stitching lines, if there are to be any, to about 1 inch (2.5 cm) below the waist-line and use an arrow to indicate the direction in which you want them folded. Pleats are traditionally folded away from the center seam in the front. However, depending on your own body contours, you may prefer to fold them the other way. Experiment with your tissue fit to see which you prefer.

Trouser pleats are usually inserted only in the front. The first pleat in pants usually extends to the crease. The crease extends from the fold line of the pleat into the middle of the front hemline.

When creating your pattern, fold the pleat/crease in the direction you want it to go and crease it from waist to hem. Be sure you maintain the correct seam allowance at the waist and, while the pleat is closed, trim along the cutting line. This will ensure the correct shape at the base of the pleat, as well as the proper hang of the crease. The grainline may need to be shifted slightly to be parallel to the crease. See Figure 14.

SKIRT WAISTBAND

To make a waistband for your skirt, use the waistband pattern from your personal pants fitting pattern. If you did not make the pants pattern, you can create a waistband easily. Like the cuff, the waistband is simply a long rectangle cut on the straight of grain the length of your waist measurement plus $1/2$ to 1 inch (1.25 to 2.5 cm) ease. Determine the finished width you would like the waistband to be, usually $1^1/4$ to $1^1/2$ inches (3 to 4 cm) wide, and double it. Then, add a buttonhole extension at one end and seam allowances to the other end and both long edges. See Figure 15. For specific instructions about how to determine proper waistband length, refer to page 95.

DESIGNING PANTS

If you wish to create palazzo pants, additional fullness can be added by uneven interior changes or by closing the darts, as in the skirt, and moving this fullness to the hem. Note that the one area you may not need to change is the length and shape of the crotch curve, which you worked so hard to perfect.

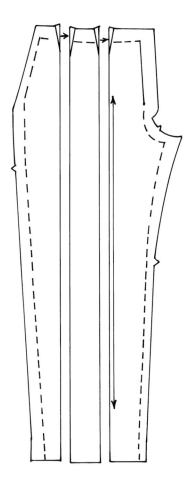

Figure 14. To add trouser pleats to the pants fitting pattern, extra width is first added from waist to hem.

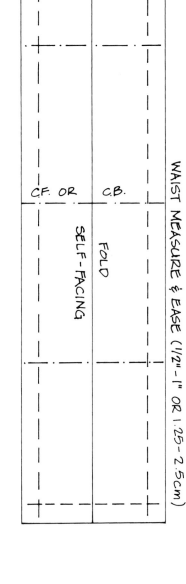

Figure 15. The waistband width is doubled to create a self-facing when folded.

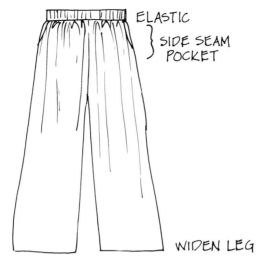

Figure 16. Pull-on pants are an easy variation of the pants fitting pattern.

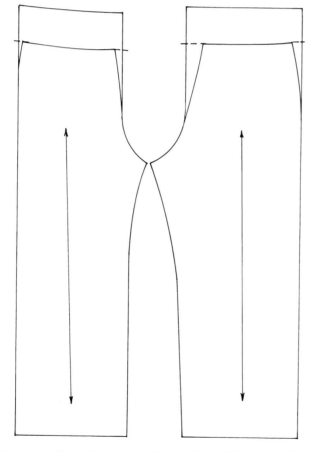

Figure 17. The side seams and waistline of the pants fitting pattern are straightened and the waistline is also extended upward, to form a casing for the elastic when folded.

However, the crotch point may need to be extended in the front and back for the fuller style. Do a tissue fit to determine if you need a looser fit in the crotch area. If you are feeling adventurous and you like the unusual look of pants that are narrow at the ankle and full at the hip, open the uneven interior changes from a hinge at the hemline up to the waist.

PULL-ON PANTS

Another way to add fullness and design ease to pants is to replace the fitted waistband and fly or side opening with an elasticized waist. See Figure 16. To do this, begin at the hipline and extend the side seamlines straight up, parallel with the grainline. Extend these seams up twice the width of the elastic plus a seam allowance. Extend the center line straight up the same amount. Draw a line to finish the top edge; it can be either straight or curved to follow the natural line of the waist. See Figure 17.

Additional width to the pant legs can be added by extending the side seams straight down from the hipline, keeping the new outseam parallel with the grainline. The inseam should also be straightened and blended from a point just above the knee straight down to the hem. See Figure 18. These changes must be made equally to the front and back pattern pieces.

PEGGED PANTS

If you wish to increase the amount of taper at the ankles, to achieve a pegged effect, redraw the inseam and outseam, subtracting an equal amount from each side at the hemline in both the front and the back. See Figure 19. To determine the absolute minimum width you need at the bottom of the pant leg to slip your foot through, measure the total distance around your ankle, from the front of the ankle around the bottom edge of the heel. For most people, this minimum clearance is approximately 13 inches (33 cm). If you want more taper, you will have to leave a slit at the bottom of the outseam to accommodate your foot.

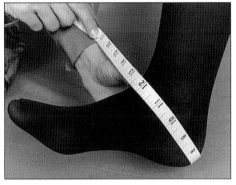

Measuring ankle to determine size of pegged pant leg at hem.

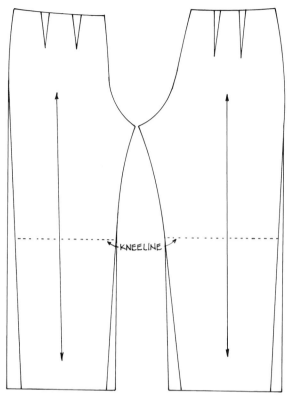

Figure 18. The inseam and outseam of the pants fitting pattern are also straightened for wider pull-on pants.

Figure 19. To create pegged pants from the fitting pattern, legs are tapered at the side seam and inseam.

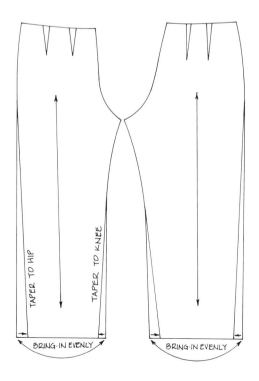

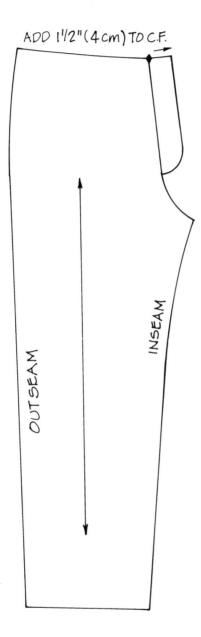

ADD 1 1/2" (4cm) TO C.F.

OUTSEAM

INSEAM

Figure 20. Adding a fly front to the pants fitting pattern.

FLY FRONT WITH ZIPPER

If you wish to add a front fly zipper to the pants pattern, make a notch at the waistline to indicate the center front. Measure 1 1/2 inches (4 cm) out from the center front, for the extension, and draw a line parallel to the center front line. This line should be 1 inch (2.5 cm) longer than the zipper you plan to insert, but not so long as to interfere with the front crotch curve. From the lower end of this new line, draw a curve back into the crotch; extend the waistline to the fly edge. See Figure 20. On one side, this extension will be folded under as a facing for the fly. The top-stitching for the zipper is usually on the right side for women's styles and the left side for men's and unisex styles.

POCKETS

Most of us like pockets in our skirts or, especially, pants. The following instructions are for two different styles.

Set-In Pockets

Creating set-in pockets along the side seamline is very easy. The pocket can be planned on the designed skirt or pants pattern and then traced onto separate pattern paper. Follow these steps:

1. On the skirt or pants pattern, place two marks at the front side seam, 1 inch (2.5 cm) and 7 1/2 inches (19 cm) below the waist point. This indicates a 6 1/2-inch (16.5-cm) pocket opening.

2. Draw the pocket pouch: From the waist point, measure toward the center front 2 to 3 inches (5 to 7.5 cm) and place a mark at the waistline seam. At the side seam, measure down from the lower mark 2¹/₂ to 3 inches (6.5 to 7.5 cm) and place another mark at this point. Now draw a line to connect the waist mark and lower side seam mark to create the pouch. See Figure 21. The line down from the waist can be parallel to the grainline and then continue either at a right angle (for a square pocket pouch) or a curve (for a rounded pocket pouch) to the lower mark on the side seam.

3. Using a fresh piece of paper, trace the pocket along the waist, side seam, and edge of the pouch, including the markings for the pocket opening.

4. Draw a grainline on the pocket, parallel to the one on the skirt or pants.

5. Add seam allowances to the pouch edge and to the waist and side seams, if needed.

6. Cut four pocket pieces out of the fashion fabric. For specific sewing instructions, consult your favorite sewing book.

Slant Pockets

A similar procedure is used to make a pattern for a slant pocket. Plan the pocket on the fitting pattern and then trace it onto fresh pattern paper. Follow these steps:

1. Begin by marking the desired slant line on the trouser or skirt front pattern; it should be at least 6¹/₂ inches (16.5 cm) long between the side and waist seamlines for the pocket opening. An easy way to draw the slant line is to measure in along the waistline from the side waist point from 1 to 3 inches (2.5 to 7.5 cm) toward the center front, avoiding any

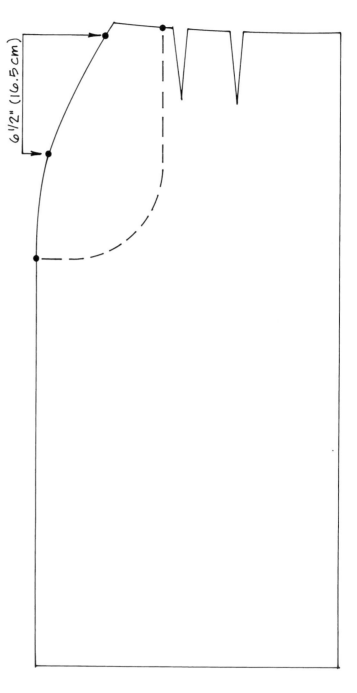

Figure 21. Tracing a pocket pouch on the skirt or pants front, to create a set-in pocket.

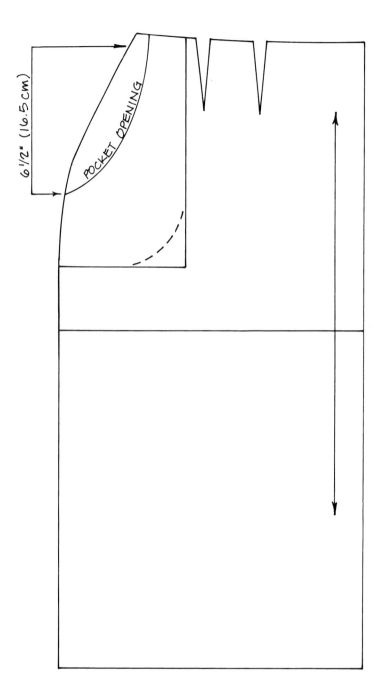

6½" (16.5 cm.)

POCKET OPENING

Figure 22. Slant pocket opening can be curved or straight; pocket pouch can be rounded or square.

pleats or darts. Make a mark at this point on the waistline. Position the end of a ruler on this point and rotate it down until the $6\frac{1}{2}$-inch (16.5-cm) point on the ruler intersects the side seam. Make a mark at this point on the side seamline and connect the two marks with a slightly curved or diagonal line. See Figure 22. Make certain that the pocket opening ends at least 2 to 3 inches (5 to 7.5 cm) above the hipline, if possible.

2. To draw the pocket pouch, measure an additional 2 to 3 inches (5 to 7.5 cm) from the pocket edge along the waistline toward the center front, excluding darts or pleats, and make a mark. Then measure down 2 to 3 inches (5 to 7.5 cm) below the side edge of the pocket and make a mark. Draw a line to connect these marks for a curved or square shape, as you did for the set-in pocket.

3. Using a fresh piece of paper, trace the slant pocket edge, and the waist, side seam, and pouch edge. Add seam allowances and grainline.

4. Place the traced pocket pattern together with another piece of paper. Cut through both layers along the waist, side seam, and pocket pouch edge. On the slant lines of the skirt/pant and pocket patterns, add seam allowances.

5. Cut along the slant line on one of the pocket patterns and on the skirt/pant front. You now have two pocket patterns: one is the back of the pocket and the other is the pocket facing.

6. Cut two of each pocket piece out of the fashion fabric and refer to your favorite sewing book for specific instructions about assembling slant pockets.

It's amazing to see the many variations you can achieve with just a few basic pattern-making techniques, isn't it? If your creativity and interest have been sparked by these experiments, you might want to learn about other exciting possibilities that exist. Even if you are relatively timid in developing your own design variations, you will be able to choose, vary, and utilize patterns much more knowledgeably now that you understand how patterns work. This familiarity with fitting and design ease, in combination with your knowledge about the very special shape of your own body, will ensure a noticeable difference in the fit of all the clothes you make. Best of all, you will wear them with newfound comfort and confidence.

Chapter Eleven

Next steps and new directions

We began this book with a question: Why another fitting book? By now, as you have journeyed toward a greater familiarity with your own figure's unique characteristics and a more thorough knowledge about the ways in which flat patterns are manipulated to become three-dimensional clothing, we hope that question has been answered to your satisfaction. But now you are faced with yet another question: Where can you go from here?

You now have the tools to achieve the perfect fit you have always dreamed about—for yourself and the lucky people for whom you sew. Fit, however, is only one part of what makes a custom-made garment worth the considerable investment it represents. Skillful sewing, attention to detail, and careful finishing are also parts of the process. As we have hinted at more than once in this book, some apparent fitting problems are actually sewing problems. Bias-cut diagonal

necklines can gap if they are stretched, buttonholes can become distorted if they are not properly underlined, and seams sewn with the incorrect stitch or stitch length, especially on the bias or on knits, can stretch out of shape. And no matter how carefully you fit the pattern and sew it together, poor pressing technique and messy seam finishing will undo all your good efforts. To perfect your sewing skills as much as you now have perfected your fitting skills, you may want to refer to the bibliography provided at the end of this book.

One of the authors is a sewing professional, the other a sewing "hobbyist." In the more than 20 years in which the hobbyist "labored in the desert," so to speak, sewing machines and products appeared on the scene that she could have only dreamed about before. Furthermore, her long-past seventh grade home economics class and the skills she had picked up from a gifted and artistic mother and in theatrical and dance costume shops often fell short of the couture-level projects she undertook. Even a careful reading and conscientious application of the pattern company's directions did not always enable her to achieve the results she envisioned.

Joining the staff at G Street Fabrics in 1990 introduced this hobbyist to books, teachers, amazing machines, and countless new notions and sewing aids—all designed to help her achieve the results she desired. Whether you are a professional or a hobbyist, you can find books, equipment, tools, and classes to inspire you and help you master ever more advanced fitting and sewing techniques. Be your own detective and search out these helpful aids in your local library, fabric store, book store, or university.

PATTERN-MAKING, DRAPING, AND GRADING

Learning how a pattern works, in the chapters of this book, may have awakened a curiosity about pattern-making, draping, and pattern-grading. We hope so. We have often worked with disappointed customers or students who can find nothing in the pattern books to match the image of a completed project they have in their mind's eye. They are understandably timid about striking out on their own, altering and mixing pattern pieces, or changing the design features of commercial pat-

terns. In Chapters Nine and Ten, we have described several ways in which you can do exactly that, so if you, too, are uncomfortable with altering your favorite fashion patterns, you might want to re-read these sections.

The intricacies of flat pattern-making, by which a sketch is transformed into a paper pattern or muslin, and finally, into a finished garment, are well beyond the scope of this modest volume. Nor can we even begin to discuss draping—how to manipulate a flat piece of muslin on a dress form to create the seams, darts, tucks, and pleats that will shape a finished design. And the grading techniques that can transform a size 10 into a size 18 are also outside the scope of this book. However, you may want to expand your horizons in all of these areas, and we encourage you to do so.

Look through the volumes listed in the bibliography to learn the difference among the three techniques and then set out on a course of self-study or learn together with your fitting buddy. If studying these more advanced skills on your own seems daunting and if you live near a good-sized fabric store, community college, or university, you might investigate whether there are any class offerings in these areas. As someone who taught high school English for nearly 20 years and who is genetically addicted to reading and book-collecting, the hobbyist is

the first to admit that even the best book is more valuable when interpreted, illuminated, and expanded by the expertise of a gifted teacher.

SETTING A NEW STANDARD

Now that you have been introduced to the joys of creating clothes that fit perfectly and are flattering to your unique figure, you will find that you now expect more from both store-bought clothing and garments you make at home. As your knowledge of good fit and sewing technique expands, you will most likely raise your expectations of quality garment construction. An anecdote might illustrate this point. One of the young models featured in this book has the good fortune to have a "sewing Mom" who, while she does not make all of her daughter's clothes, has always created special event garments for her, her sister, and her sister-in-law. Late one evening, the college-age daughter and her roommate stopped by for a fitting of a new one-of-a-kind winter formal gown. As mother and daughter fussed over small details of fit, eliminating the same types of wrinkles, stress points, and baggy sections you have fussed over during the fitting sessions in this book, the roommate was astounded. Having always been at the mercy of ready-to-wear selections, she had no idea it was possible to have clothes that fit so perfectly. You, too, will be astounded when the first fashion garments you make, using your basic dress and pants fitting patterns, fit you perfectly. Your outlook on clothing will be changed forever.

From this point on, everything in your closet will be labeled B.F.P. (Before Fitting Pattern) and A.F.P. (After Fitting Pattern). You just won't be able to wear the dress that strains or gaps along the bustline, whose waistline lands either above or below yours, whose buttoned front refuses to stay closed at the bust, and whose pockets gap awkwardly at the hip—until you adjust it or make it again, perfectly. In fact, many of those B.F.P. garments, whether purchased in a store or created in your sewing room, will now be put to the fit test. If they don't pass, they can be adjusted to fit, if not perfectly, at least acceptably.

The philosophers, indeed, have told us that self-knowledge is the beginning of wisdom. Along the journey to wisdom, one of the most important lessons you have learned is that the very best fit is as unique as you are and, to a large degree, achieved before you ever take scissors to fabric and certainly long before the garment is sewn together. Those extra few minutes comparing the commercial fashion pattern to your fitting pattern and transferring the basic corrections to your fashion pattern will make an unbelievable difference in how you look and feel in your clothes. You will even see a difference in how others react to you—with admiration for your flawless appearance and flattering sense of style.

You don't believe that such simple steps as those we have outlined can make that much difference? A final anecdote will prove that they can, and do. While the "sewing expert" author was teaching her four-day Total Fit class at G Street Fabrics, the "hobbyist" author happened to be wearing a simple but flattering dress created from her fitting pattern, with the modification of a gently flared skirt. The class members all remarked on the beautiful fit of this dress when she walked through the classroom. On the next day, she wore a princess line dress made from a commercial pattern that she altered by using her basic pattern and following the techniques described in Chapter Nine. She received a number of compliments on that dress, too, and at least one inquiry about whether she had lost some weight. In short, the little bit of effort she put into her newly made clothes made a big difference!

Once you've achieved the perfect fit, you will love wearing garments that show off your best characteristics to their greatest advantage—and others will notice! You'll wear your clothes with well-deserved confidence, knowing they fit perfectly, feel wonderful, and look sensational.

Appendix

Finding a fitting buddy

The organizations listed below can provide information about local chapters in your area. Young sewers (up to age 18) interested in locating other youngsters who sew might contact their local chapters or councils of the Girl Scouts, Campfire Girls, or 4H. Older sewers (age 50 and older) might contact their local senior citizen's organizations and centers.

In addition, watch for notices published in PTA, neighborhood association, and church or synagogue bulletins, or place a notice in these bulletins about your interest in contacting a potential fitting buddy. World Wide Web surfers can check in with on-line chat groups and bulletin boards.

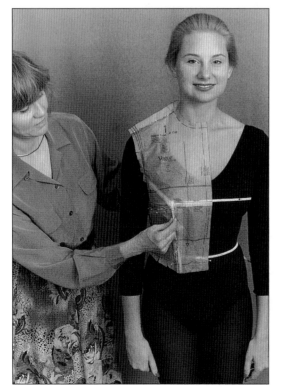

American Sewing Guild
Dept. SN Box 8476
Medford, OR 97504
541/772-4059

Handweaver's Guild of America, Inc.
3327 Duluth Hwy, Suite #201
Duluth, GA 30136-3373
770/495-7702

The Bishop Method of Clothing
    Construction Council, Inc.
Lynn Hunter
3310 North Vernon St.
Arlington, VA 22207
703/241-0123

Wearable Art Connection
Cheryl Trustrud-White
23344 Park Hacienda
Calabasas, CA 91302-1715
818/222-5958

Annotated Bibliography

BASIC SEWING AND PATTERN SELECTION SKILLS

Betzina, Sandra. *No Time to Sew*. Emmaus, Pennsylvania: Rodale Press, 1996.
Comes with patterns for a wardrobe designed to accommodate sewing time constraints and the changing nature of our figures as we age.

Butterick Company. *Vogue/Butterick Step-By-Step Guide to Sewing*. New York: Simon & Schuster, 1994.
Written for the beginning to average sewer, it replaces the old *Vogue Fitting Book*.

Farro, Rita. *Life Is Not a Dress Size*. Radnor, Pennsylvania: Chilton Book Company, 1996.
Choosing a wardrobe for the larger-sized woman.

Long, Connie. *Easy Guide to Sewing Blouses*. Newtown, Connecticut: The Taunton Press, 1997.
Basic to intermediate book written by one of G Street's most popular sewing teachers.

McWilliams, Laurie. *Blouses, Skirts, and Tops*. New York: Sterling Publishing Co., 1996.
Includes tips on using the serger to perform necessary tasks.

Podolak, Cecelia. *Easy Guide to Sewing Jackets*. Newtown, Connecticut: The Taunton Press, 1995.
Covers techniques for constructing a collarless jacket using fusible interfacings rather than traditional padstitching.

Reader's Digest. *Complete Guide to Sewing, Revised Edition*. Pleasantville, New York: Reader's Digest, 1995.
Most comprehensive basic book, which also offers much to the intermediate and advanced sewer.

Shaeffer, Claire. *Claire Shaeffer's Fabric Sewing Guide*. Radnor, Pennsylvania: Chilton Book Company, 1994.
Thorough discussion of garment fabric types, content, stitching tips, and care.

Simplicity Pattern Company. *Simplicity's Simply the Best Sewing Book*. New York: The Simplicity Pattern Company, 1988.
Includes some home decorating techniques as well as garment sewing.

Singer Sewing Reference Library. *Sewing Essentials*. Minnetonka, Minnesota: Cy DeCosse Publishing, 1984.
Good introduction to the sewing machine, commercial patterns, and basic sewing techniques.

Tilton, Marcy. *Easy Guide to Sewing Skirts*. Newtown, Connecticut: The Taunton Press, 1995.
Includes directions for adding a lining to an unlined skirt pattern and making simple side seam pockets.

COUTURE AND TAILORING TECHNIQUES

The following titles are suggested for the intermediate level sewer who is ready to advance her skills to the couture level.

Amaden-Crawford, Connie. *A Guide to Fashion Sewing*. 2nd ed. New York: Fairchild Publications, 1994.

Cabrera, Roberto, and Patricia Flaherty Meyers. *Classic Tailoring Techniques: A Construction Guide for Women's Wear*. New York: Fairchild Publications, 1984.

Carr, Roberta. *Couture: The Art of Fine Sewing*. Portland, Oregon: Palmer/Pletsch, 1994.
A peek inside couture garments.

Coffin, David. *Shirtmaking: Developing Skills for Fine Sewing.* Newtown, Connecticut: The Taunton Press, 1993.
Men's shirts, including collars, yokes, set-in sleeves, plackets, buttonholes, and more.

Flury, Mary Ellen. *Tailoring Ladies Jackets.* Annapolis, Maryland: Parker Publishing, 1996.
Covers traditional and modern tailoring techniques.

Shaeffer, Claire. *Couture Sewing Techniques.* Newtown, Connecticut: The Taunton Press, 1993.
Illustrated with photographs of both the exteriors and interiors of couture garments.

———. *High-Fashion Sewing Secrets from the World's Best Designers.* Emmaus, Pennsylvania: Rodale Press, 1997.
More adventures in the couture sewing room, covering collars to hem.

PATTERN-MAKING, DRAPING, AND GRADING TECHNIQUES
These titles are designed for the serious student of fashion design and construction. They are probably best found in college and university book stores that offer a Fashion Design and/or Textile major. Also available from G Street Fabrics.

Amaden-Crawford, Connie. *The Art of Fashion Draping.* 2nd ed. New York: Fairchild Publications, 1996.
How to create clothing without a flat pattern, simply by manipulating fabric on a dress form.

Armstrong, H. *Patternmaking for Fashion Design.* 2nd ed. New York: HarperCollins College Division, 1993.
The standard college text for pattern-making.

Cloake, Dawn. *Fashion Design on the Stand.* London: B.T. Batsford, Ltd., 1996.
How to drape a basic dress design with conventionally placed darts, as well as interesting design options.

Doyle, Tracy. *Patterns from Finished Clothes.* A Sterling/Lark Book. New York: Sterling Publishing Co., 1997.
Written by a G Street Fabrics teacher. Explains how to take finished clothes, whether ready-to-wear or made from discontinued patterns, and re-create them.

Hollen, Norma R., and Carolyn J. Kundel. *Pattern Making by the Flat Pattern Method.* 7th ed. New York: Macmillan, 1993.
Designed to be a college text, this book is more detailed and advanced than the Armstrong text listed above.

Kopp, Ernestine, Vittorina Rolfo, Beatrice Zelin, and Lee Gross. *How to Draft Basic Patterns.* 4th ed. New York: Fairchild Fashion & Merchandising Group, 1996.
Designed as a college text.

Price, Jeanne, and Bernard Zamkoff. *Grading Techniques for Fashion Design.* New York: Fairchild Publications, 1996.
G Street Fabrics students use this as their text for Sally McCann's pattern-grading course.

Zamkoff, Bernard, and Jeanne Price. *Basic Pattern Skills for Fashion Design.* New York: Fairchild Publications, 1987.
G Street Fabrics students use this as their text for Sally McCann's pattern-making course.

———. *Creative Pattern Skills for Fashion Design.* New York: Fairchild Publications, 1990.
Helps advanced students who have mastered their basic book create unique garments.

Zangrillo, Frances Leto. *Fashion Design for the Plus-Size.* New York: Fairchild Publications, 1990.
Pattern-making techniques for larger sizes.

Dedicated to the G Street Fabrics "Misfits" and the memory of Sue Gursey, who put it all in perspective when she said, "I am doing this for the millions of women who look like me."

Acknowledgments

The authors gratefully acknowledge their debts to the following:

First and foremost, to the G Street Fabrics customers and students, for showing us the need for this book and for collaborating with us in finding the solutions to so many problems.

To all our co-workers at G Street Fabrics and to the Greenzaid family members, for their magnificent support and encouragement.

To the G Street Fabrics "Misfits," for their generosity of spirit and their unfailing efforts to "get the perfect fit."

To G Street Fabrics sewing specialist and instructor Nancy Fève, for sharing her expertise, especially about fitting Burda patterns, and for her meticulous and thoughtful reviewing of the text.

To Rose Gerstner, a colleague who quite intently reviewed the text.

To the models who bravely revealed their "before" and "after" garments, and their figures, in front of the camera: Chris Beckley, Nancy Fève, Dottie Gordon, Gard Hirschfeld, Marietta Houk, Farideh Jahanbin, Amanda Ladd, Bridget Morris, Mary B. Morris, Andrea Munn, Marisa Munn, Tracy Munn, Elizabeth Searle, and Joy F. Virden.

To our husbands and families, for tolerating our many working weekends and innumerable missed or carry-out meals, and for always being there to help solve all kinds of problems, from legal questions to recalcitrant computers.

To Sue Barnabee of *Sew News*, for information about sewing organizations.

To our editor, Kate Mathews, and the superb professionals at Lark Books, for their encouragement, expertise, and commitment to this project.

Index